CRITICAL READING AND THINKING SKILLS

BOOK ONE

Critical Reading

AND THINKING SKILLS

BOOK ONE

Barnes • Fischer

Phoenix Learning Resources
St. Louis • New York

Authors' Acknowledgment

We wish to thank our wives, Joan and Ann, for their patience and assistance in the completion of this book.

Cover and interior page design: Pencil Point Studio
Illustrations: Cindy Hernandez and Damien Garcia

Copyright © 2001 By Phoenix Learning Resources, Inc. All Rights Reserved. Printed in the United States of America. No part of this publication may be reproduced, stored in a retrieval system, or transmitted, in any form or by any means, electronic, mechanical, photocopying, recording, or otherwise, without the prior written permission of the publisher.

ISBN: 0-7915-1600-8

1 2 3 4 5 6 7 8 9 0 DBH 07 06 05 04 03 02 01 00

About the Authors

Don Barnes

Don Barnes recently retired from Ball State University, Muncie, Indiana after completing a teaching career in the public schools of Iowa, Minnesota, and the Island of Guam. Dr. Barnes has conducted extensive research and careful analyses of children's competencies in mastering fundamental reading comprehension skills. These studies have subsequently provided a firm foundation for the development of a wide range of reading instructional programs. These studies and descriptions of these investigations have been published in eight countries throughout the world. He recently served As an educational consultant at universities in Taiwan. Dr. Barnes has published seventy-three books related to language skills and reading comprehension over the past twenty years.

Wyman E. Fischer

Wyman E. Fischer is professor emeritus of psychology and chairman emeritus of the Department of Educational Psychology at Ball State University, Muncie, Indiana. He received his Ph.D. in Educational Psychology from Southern Illinois University, Carbondale, Illinois. In addition to teaching courses in human development, psychological evaluation, and neuropsychology, Dr. Fischer has published numerous research articles and several book chapters on brain functions as they relate to language learning activities. He was licensed as a health services provider in psychology and completed numerous psychological evaluations of children with learning disabilities. Prior to beginning his university teaching and administration career, Dr. Fischer served as teacher and principal of an elementary school in Illinois.

CONTENTS

UNIT 1:
DISTINGUISHING BETWEEN FACT AND OPINION 1

Dying by Degrees 3
Row, Row, Row Your Boat 5
The Jesse James Gang 6
The Queen of the Fire-eaters 7
Ships of the Desert 8
Helen Keller 9
The Real Robinson Crusoe 11
The Mad Monk of Russia 12
The Greatest Escape Artist of All Time 13
A Home Away from Home 15

UNIT 2:
DRAWING VALID CONCLUSIONS 16

Shackelton's Trails 17
Fireflies for Sale 18
The Indian Rope Trick 19
The Knife Swallowing Incident 20
Cheiro the Great 22
Using Magic Rods 24
The Discoverer of America 25
A Prisoner and a Shoemaker 26

UNIT 3:
CLASSIFYING OBJECTS, PEOPLE, THINGS, AND EVENTS 27

Odd Habits of Bees 29
Swallowed by a Whale 31
The Will to Succeed 34
An Army of Animals 36
Do Animals Predict Atmospheric Changes? 38
A Prisoner in Parliament 40

UNIT 4:
RECOGNIZING SEQUENCES   42

Desert Shrimp.. 43
Bee Messages.. 43
Animals with Egg Teeth 43
Water, Water Everywhere 43
Mary Lindley Murray.. 44
Nancy Hart 45
Nellie Bly.. 46
Is Hypnosis a Trick?.. 47
The Man with the Magic Touch................................. 49
Booker T. Washington 51

UNIT 5:
SELECTING CRITERIA FOR USE IN MAKING JUDGMENTS   52

The Great Escape 53
Teaching Big Cats 55
Survival in the Arctic 57
Dangerous Superhuman Achievements......................... 59
An Indian Woman Leads the Way 61
Adrift in the Atlantic Ocean.................................... 63
Inventing a New Language..................................... 65
The First Worldwide Automobile Race 67

UNIT 6:   DETECTING ASSUMPTIONS   69

The Most Misunderstood Animal in the World 71
Dealing with Stress.. 73
Can Dreams Predict the Future? 75
Giants of the Deep 77
Ballooning to the North Pole 79
A Simple "No" Started a Revolution 80

UNIT 7:
REVIEW: PUTTING IT ALL TOGETHER   83

Faithful Forever 84
The Song That Wrote Itself 87
A Magic Trick.. 90
The Man with the X-ray Mind................................... 93
Bicycling Across the English Channel 96
Cinque Wins His Freedom..................................... 100

To the Student

Arturo Toscanini, a famous orchestra leader, once said, "I kissed my first girl and smoked my first cigarette on the same day. I haven't had time for tobacco since." Obviously, he preferred girls to smoking. You, too, are likely to prefer some things over others. Many of your friends may like trendy clothes or sports. Others may prefer the chat room on the internet, hobbies, or camping. Although people's interests differ, just about everybody wants to be clever and smart.

Woody Allen once commented, "I'm not afraid to die. I just don't want to be there when it happens." That would be quite a trick—skipping your own funeral. We can't promise that Critical Reading and Thinking Skills, Books 1 and 2 will make you this clever, but the skills in these books will certainly help you make smarter decisions.

We all recognize that it is our higher level thinking and reasoning that makes us different from animals. Other creatures may have keener senses, swifter legs, or longer life spans. However, they cannot match our thinking skills.

The stories and activities in these books are carefully chosen to help you strengthen twelve important thinking skills. These are basic to most of the activities you will face in school and on the job.

We think you will enjoy the stories. They describe unusual creatures and unforgettable people. They even tell about mysterious happenings, historical events, and unusual incidents in the lives of the famous people.

The stories and activities in these books will convince you that learning new skills can be both enjoyable and important to your personal success. Employers all over America want workers who can read intelligently and find better ways of solving problems.

If you have time, write us a note about these stories. We would like to hear from you. Send your comments to the publisher.

The Authors

UNIT 1
Distinguishing Between FACT AND OPINIONS

> **Words you'll need to know...**
> **confirmed** proven to be accurate
> **defendant** person on trial
> **documented** careful record of events
> **opinion** a belief not backed up by proof
> **verified** proven to be true

If you have ever seen TV shows or movies about police work or detectives you know how important it is to "get the facts." Detectives can't arrest a person simply because he looks guilty. In addition, a jury can't convict a **defendant** because he seems to have committed a crime. Lawyers have to prove that the defendant is guilty. They need facts. A fact is a statement about a person, object, or event that has been **verified** and **documented**. It has been observed, usually by several people, and proven to be true through careful examination.

We frequently hear people say that they have the true facts or the real facts. This doesn't make sense. One fact isn't truer than another fact because they have both been proven to be true.

Facts give specific information. The dog is in the yard. The house is white. The tree is cone-shaped. These are very definite statements. Anyone who questions this kind of specific information can go see for themselves.

There can be at least two problems in establishing facts:

1. In discussing the color of the house, people may not all agree on what "white" is. Some may decide that the house is "ivory" or "cream" rather than white. In discussing the shape of the tree, some may say it is heart-shaped or round rather than cone-shaped.

2. Second, there is the difference between personal and public information.

When a friend tells you about a dream or feelings he or she has toward a classmate, there is no way you can observe these experiences directly. These dreams or feelings are your friend's personal knowledge. On the other hand, there are many events that can be observed by more than one person. If you are told that the visiting team has arrived, you can go check to see if it is true. We become more confident about our observations when they are confirmed by others.

See if you can distinguish between personal knowledge and public information. Which two of the four statements below depend most on personal knowledge?

1. Jack felt uneasy about taking Joan out.
2. Tim and Larry went to the lab.
3. Susan was enjoying her Spanish class.
4. Rosa could not get her car started.

If you chose one and three, you are correct.

Statements of **opinion** are very different from statements of fact. When people express an opinion, they really tell us what they prefer or like or dislike. Opinions are judgments about what they feel is good, useful, pleasing, disagreeable, useless, or bad. People express opinions about many of the things they experience–friends, classes, music, sports, inventions, politics, and community events. It is not unusual for a person to be completely amazed at the choices made by his or her friends. Their opinions about clothing, music, and out-of-school activities may seem astonishing.

Can you distinguish between statements of fact and statements of opinion? Put "fact" in the blanks before factual statements and "opinion" in the blanks next to those that express opinions. Remember, a factual statement is one that can be proven true or false.

_____ 1. Jane is the captain of the soccer team.

_____ 2. Alan lives in the fourth house.

_____ 3. Rosa is my sister.

_____ 4. Aaron is the cutest guy in the class.

_____ 5. Everyone should try hard in school.

_____ 6. Football is the most exciting sport.

_____ 7. The United States is the greatest country.

_____ 8. Everyone should help with the project.

_____ 9. Dogs make better pets than cats.

_____ 10. Judy has one sister.

Dying by Degrees

Words you'll need to know...
bail throw water out of a boat
Communists people who believe factories and farms should be owned by the government
coral reef a rock-like island in the ocean
merchants people who sell goods

Have you ever wondered what it would be like to watch yourself slowing dying in a strange, lonely place? How would you react? Would you try to talk yourself into being brave? Would you close your eyes and dream that things would soon be better? Would you pray? When things are very bad, we sometimes turn out to be braver than we thought we could be. On the other hand, we might just fall apart.

This is the story of a 17-year-old Vietnamese girl. Her name was Tran Hue Hue. She and her family sought to flee their homeland in 1978. Her father was a watch seller in a Vietnamese village.

At the time, the **Communists** greatly disliked **merchants**. The officials took all of her father's watches, and he had no way of making a living. Hue and her family decided their only hope was to flee the country.

They made a farewell visit to their ancestors' tombs, burned incense at the altars, and asked their forgiveness for leaving their homeland. After that, they gathered all their belongings. They sold what they could for gold. Then they used the gold to bribe the owner of a boat to take them down the river at night.

There were fifty people on the boat. It rained so hard that the adults had to **bail** continuously to keep the boat from filling with water. Three large ships sailed near them without stopping. Finally, their small boat hit a **coral reef** and sank.

The next morning the passengers saw a large white ship nearby. They thought they might be rescued. They soon discovered that the white ship was also wrecked and it was abandoned.

Those who could dive for oysters around the reef could eat for a few days, but they did not share the oysters with the others. They noticed a few ships in the distance and burned clothing to get attention. None of the ships stopped.

The people in the group became thin and sick. Many looked like dried corpses. The children soon died of diarrhea. The people who were still alive tried to float boards out into the waves.

A message was attached to each board saying, "We are 12 people left on a coral reef. Please help us. SOS."

Two weeks later there were only seven of them left. By now people were having dreams during which they imagined that a ship was coming. The only source of food was sea gulls. When one would settle on a railing, the survivors would throw a blanket over it. Some nights they caught as many as twenty gulls. They would dry some for the days when they caught none at all.

Finally, all of the passengers except Hue were dead. She was frightened by her loneliness. There were days when she didn't catch a single gull. She could barely crawl. She would lie on her stomach and dream of food. One night she dreamt that her dead brothers were saying, "Wake up, Hue, a ship is coming!"

As daylight broke the next day, Hue thought she heard an engine. She stood up for the first time in almost two weeks. There was a ship! She waved a white shirt as it came closer. As nineteen men came on board, Hue pointed to herself and said "Vietnam." They replied "Filipinos."

They used sign language to tell her to follow them to their ship. Her legs gave way, and the seamen had to carry her to the fishing boat.

The strangers fed Hue and laughed when she gulped her food. Hue was taken to Palawan Island. She saw a wall calendar dated February 18, 1979. She wondered how she could have lived so long. A dark, thin man asked her in Vietnamese, "Are you Hue?" Then he added, "I'm also a Vietnamese refugee. Don't worry." Hue could not find words to express her happiness. She could see better days ahead.

Questions and Discussion

1. Hue had many experiences. Some of these can be described as factual. Others can better be expressed as opinions. Write fact or opinion beside each statement below.

    _____ a. Hue was the only survivor among fifty refugees.

    _____ b. The ship carrying the refugees should not have left port.

    _____ c. The refugees died of hunger and disease.

    _____ d. There were too many people on the boat.

    _____ e. Hue was a brave person.

    _____ f. Hue was lucky.

2. Hue applied for entry into the United States. Write a recommendation below expressing your feelings about admitting Hue to our country.

    _____

    _____

    _____

    _____

    _____

Row, Row, Row Your Boat

Words you'll need to know...
clunky awkward, cumbersome
editorial statement of opinion of a newspaper
sea-lanes routes traveled by ships
seaman a sailor

Have you ever fished from a row boat? Have you tried to row the boat across a lake or stream? If you have, you know that rowing a boat is quite difficult. The oars and the boat are hard to control. The first time you try it you will probably go in circles. It is hard to pull evenly on both oars and they steer the boat.

Two people, and only people, have successfully rowed across the Atlantic Ocean from America to Europe. There may have been others who tried and failed. Several **seamen** have used sails in crossing to Europe or had engine-driven boats. Only George Harbo and Frank Samuelson did it using their own arms.

On June 6, 1896, Harbo and Samuelson rowed out of New York harbor in a boat only eighteen feet long. It was a **clunky**, heavy, wooden boat, twice the weight of today's sleek aluminum boats. It had no mast to hold on to during raging storms. They did have sixty gallons of water, five pairs of oars, and plenty of canned food.

Harbo and Samuelson chose a travel route just south of the normal **sea-lanes** traveled by freighters and passenger ships. These vessels offered them their only hope of being rescued if their boat broke up or sank. They had no radio contact with people on land or on the sea.

Harbo and Samuelson planned a strict schedule. They expected to row fifty-four miles a day and they kept to the schedule. Each man rowed eighteen hours a day, mostly at night. They allowed five hours for rest and one hour for eating.

Fortunately, the two fearless seamen did not encounter big storms or heavy winds. On July 15, however, they boarded a freighter and got fresh food, then sped on their way. On August 1, fifty-six days after leaving New York, Harbo and Samuelson landed on the Isles of Scilly off the coast of England. They had accomplished the impossible, and no one has ever challenged their record.

Questions and Discussion

1. Decide which statements below are factual and which sentences express opinions. Put fact or opinion in the blanks.

   _____ a. Harbo and Samuelson took unnecessary chances.

   _____ b. Harbo and Samuelson made plans before leaving New York harbor.

   _____ c. Harbo and Samuelson were clever.

   _____ d. Harbo and Samuelson completed a voyage that will never be repeated.

   _____ e. No rowers have been successful in duplicating their achievement.

2. On a separate sheet write a brief **editorial** giving your opinion of their trip.

The Jesse James Gang

Words you'll need to know...

caravan traveling line of wagons, trucks, or animals

raids quick attacks

The Jesse James gang roamed the Old West looking for treasure to steal. They traveled from North Dakota to the Texas border. On one of their **raids** near the Mexican border, Jesse, his men, and his brother Frank captured a **caravan** carrying gold bars. The gold was worth a fortune, and the gang knew they had to hide it quickly. News of their success would soon spread, and other outlaws would be looking for a chance to steal it.

The gang could not travel very fast with the heavy wagons of gold. Jesse decided to travel by night and seek cover in the Wichita Mountains to the north. When the gang finally reached the mountains in the present state of Oklahoma, they were tired and eager to find a safe place to hide their gold. They carefully buried their treasure. They made certain that there were no wagon tracks or other marks to give away their secret.

Some years later Jesse James was killed, and Frank gave up his life of crime. It was then that Frank decided to go back to the Wichita Mountains for the gold. He bought a farm near the mountains and began his search but he never found the treasure. Other people have also tried to find the gold. As far as anybody knows, the treasure is still hidden near Frank's farm.

Questions and Discussion

1. List three facts given in the story.

   _____

   _____

   _____

2. What is your guess or opinion regarding what happened to the hidden gold?

   _____

   _____

   _____

   _____

The Queen of the Fire-eaters

Words you'll need to know...
demonstrated to show
performers people who put on acts

In early days when there was no TV or movies, **performers** would go from village to village doing exciting tricks to entertain people. At the beginning of the 1800s, fire-eaters performed by chewing live coals and holding red-hot iron bars in their hands. Jo Guardelli was the queen of the fire-eaters.

Guardelli was born in Italy about 1780. She toured England in 1818 and was a great success. She was popular with audiences because she **demonstrated** her amazing powers time and time again.

Guardelli used six materials in her act: acid, boiling oil, hot wax, melted metal, hot metal, and lit candles. For her acid act, she held acid in her mouth and then spit it out on iron. The powerful acid would make the iron give off an orange smoke. Her oil act was just frightening. Before actually putting oil in her mouth, she'd prove it was boiling hot by using it to fry an egg. After this, she'd go on to hot wax that she'd pour into her mouth. Someone would then make a seal on it and show it to the audience. For her melted metal act, Guardelli would dip her fingers in it, put it in her mouth, and spit out round coin-like pieces. Hot metal was no challenge at all to her. She would jump barefoot on it and pat her arms and feet with a red-hot shovel. No burns ever showed. Her final act involved lit candles. These were passed under her arms and feet. The flames would surround her toes!

Guardelli seems to have earned her fame. She remained cool with very hot materials. How she did it is still a mystery.

Questions and Discussion

1. Which of the following statements deal with facts? Which express opinions? Put fact or opinion in each blank.

   _____ a. Jo Guardelli took too many chances.

   _____ b. No burns ever showed on Guardelli.

   _____ c. Guardelli was an excellent performer.

   _____ d. We should have more show people today.

   _____ e. Guardelli toured England.

   _____ f. Other people should have learned her tricks.

2. Did Guardelli have magic powers? Express your opinion.

Helen Keller

Words you'll need to know...
breakthrough a sudden advance
expressive making known through movement
frustration condition of not achieving a purpose or fulfilling a desire
inspiration encouragement
productive yielding favorable or useful results
rational having a sound mind, sane

Have you ever thought about how important language is to your life? Helen Keller's life story illustrates clearly how a command of language can change an uninteresting, bitter existence into an exciting, **productive** adventure.

When Helen Keller was 19 months old she was struck with an illness that left her deaf and blind. Unable to hear or see, Helen was also unable to speak. Frustrated at not being able to communicate, Helen became uncontrollable. In her more **rational** moments, however, she used signals to communicate. To ask for ice cream, she would turn the handle of an imaginary freezer. For bread and butter, she would go through the motions of cutting and spreading. She pretended to put on glasses when she wanted to refer to her father.

The turning point in Helen's life came the day her family hired Annie Sullivan as Helen's teacher. Annie was an extraordinary person. She was very intelligent, kind, and determined to help Helen learn about the world. Annie knew that Helen's rages came from **frustration**, not stubbornness. Annie was anxious to teach Helen to communicate through sign language, the **expressive** hand language for deaf people.

Months went by. During this time, Annie hand-spelled thousands of words for Helen. But how could she make Helen understand that the letters stood for words and the words represented objects? Finally, the **breakthrough** came. Annie had taken Helen to the pump to draw some water. As the water flowed over Helen's right hand, Annie spelled W-A-T-E-R into Helen's left hand. She did it over and over again. All at once, Helen stood dumbfounded. Annie repeated the process. Helen's face lit up. She understood. The letters represented the cold liquid that was flowing over her hand. Helen returned to the house in a fever of excitement, touching everything as she moved, visibly seeking their names. Within the space of a few hours, she had added 30 new words to her vocabulary. From that point on, her education moved quickly. Eventually, Helen became a world-famous teacher and lecturer. She was an **inspiration** to people the world over.

DISTINGUISHING BETWEEN FACT AND OPINIONS

Questions and Discussion

1. Write fact or opinion beside the statements below.

    _____ a. Helen Keller was patient.

    _____ b. When Helen Keller was nineteen months old she became ill.

    _____ c. Annie Sullivan was wise.

    _____ d. Annie Sullivan taught Helen.

    _____ e. Helen Keller was known to other deaf and blind people.

    _____ f. Helen Keller became world-famous.

2. In your opinion how did Helen Keller inspire people the world over?

_____
_____
_____
_____
_____
_____
_____
_____
_____
_____
_____
_____
_____
_____
_____
_____
_____
_____

The Real Robinson Crusoe

Words you'll need to know...
first mate officer ranked just below the captain on a ship
infested overrun, covered
uninhabited no people live there

The famous story of Robinson Crusoe by Daniel Defoe is based upon a real-life adventure! For four years, a Scottish sailor named Alexander Selkirk actually lived on a small island off the coast of Chile in the South Pacific.

When he was a teenager, Selkirk became a sailor and took part in several sailing expeditions to the South Pacific. In 1704 he was the **first mate** of the English vessel *Cinque Ports*. Selkirk was a skillful seaman but he was often stubborn. He quarreled with the captain of the boat. The captain became so angry that he left Selkirk on an **uninhabited** island.

Selkirk pleaded to be taken back on board the ship, but his pleas were ignored. He was not rescued until four years later by a British ship in January of 1709. When he was abandoned, Selkirk had been left with clothes, a hatchet, a pistol, gunpowder, and bullets. Although his gunpowder soon gave out, he learned to capture the wild goats on the island by running them down. He ate goat meat and made clothes from goat skins.

The weather was generally quite good. There was only a little frost and hail in June and July (winter in the Southern Hemisphere). The summers (from December to March) were hot but they were not unbearable. The island was heavily **infested** with rats, but Selkirk solved this problem by taming stray cats and training them to catch the rodents.

Selkirk kept healthy by improving his home and by making pets of the animals. When he was rescued he had many problems. For one thing, he had difficulty making himself understood. He had simply not spoken English for too long. In addition, he had become so used to simple food that he had little interest in English meals.

Questions and Discussion

1. Mark the statements below to indicate whether they are facts or opinions.

   _____ a. Alexander Selkirk was very clever.

   _____ b. Alexander Selkirk was a skillful seaman.

   _____ c. Alexander Selkirk captured goats.

   _____ d. Alexander Selkirk should not have argued with the captain..

2. Give your opinion regarding the conflict between Alexander Selkirk and the captain. Which of the two was more at fault?

The Mad Monk of Russia

Words you'll need to know...
anxieties tensions, fright
commanding strong, attracting attention
hypnotic put into a trance
prophet can predict happenings

One of the most unusual people who ever lived in Russia was Grigori Rasputin. He was born in 1871 into a poor peasant family. When he was twelve an event occurred that changed his life. He and his brother were swimming in the Tura River. Both boys were pulled beneath the surface. A peasant dragged the boys out but only Rasputin lived. He believed his life had been spared so he could do something special. Seven years later, he became a wandering preacher. He claimed to have healing powers and the ability to predict the future.

Rasputin's **hypnotic** powers brought him attention everywhere he went. People were attracted to him and they listened carefully to what he said. He was lucky enough to be befriended by important people who introduced him to the Russian emperor, known as the czar.

Rasputin's real claim to fame occurred at the court of Czar Nicholas II. The son of the czar, Prince Alexis, suffered from hemophilia. This is a rare disease that causes severe bleeding. Rasputin appeared to greatly improve the boy's condition. Because of this the prince's mother, Alexandra, believed that Rasputin was a saint.

Rasputin used his powers on Alexis, weaving tales and filling the darkened room with his **commanding** voice. The young prince was fascinated. Rasputin assured the boy that his pain would ease and his bleeding would stop. Alexis became calm and lay quietly. Soon his bleeding stopped altogether. Rasputin seemed to be performing miracles. In reality he was simply diminishing the flow of blood in the boy's body by reducing the child's fears and **anxieties**.

A group of Russian nobles became jealous of Rasputin's power. They also suspected him of disloyalty to the mother country. On the night of December 29, 1916, they killed the strange **prophet**.

Questions and Discussion

1. List three facts we know about Rasputin.
   _____
   _____
   _____

2. What is your opinion of this unusual man?
   _____
   _____

The Greatest Escape Artist of All Time

Words you'll need to know...
contract make smaller
controversial something that causes people to express strong feelings
fascinated aroused great interest, attraction
straitjacket a binding that keeps people from moving

Over one hundred years ago Harry Houdini's amazing escape acts **fascinated** millions of people all over the world. There were no prisons or handcuffs or chains that could hold him. His performances were so unbelievable that many who saw his acts thought Houdini had supernatural powers.

Houdini could open any lock in the world in a few minutes. Once Houdini was invited to escape from England's famous Scotland Yard. The prison superintendent, Mr. Melville, placed Houdini's arms around a pillar, handcuffed him, and left. Before Melville could leave the building, Houdini freed himself and joined him on the way out. A little later, the most famous locksmiths from around Europe presented him with what they considered their most foolproof locks. They had worked on them for countless years. Houdini opened the locks so quickly that the master locksmiths hardly had time to sit down before it was all over.

Houdini escaped from jails in Liverpool, England, Amsterdam, and every large city in the United States. The plain fact was that he could enter or leave any room or prison cell anywhere at any time. Once he was placed in a **straitjacket**, bound with chains, and hung upside down on a rope in front of thousands of people. In no time at all he was bowing to the audience.

On one occasion Houdini was handcuffed, chained, and sealed inside a wooden box. The box was then lowered into the East River in New York City. He freed himself and emerged from the water within two minutes.

How did he manage to escape so often? His success was based on two things. First, Houdini had amazing strength throughout his body. From his early youth in Appleton, Wisconsin, on, he practiced body control. His fingers had the strength of pliers. He could bend iron bars and **contract** his muscles so that his arms and legs could slip through the handcuffs and chains that held him. Second, he often used clever tricks to free himself. When he was placed in the wooden box in the East River, the handcuffs were fake. He also took small nail cutters with him. He cut just enough nails to slip out. These were replaced quietly by carpenters behind stage.

Although Houdini used tricks, he was always in real danger during his acts. He seemed to enjoy taking risks. He would sometimes jump from one airplane to another 3,000 feet above the ground. As usual, he was handcuffed during the entire act! Just before he died in 1927, Houdini made notes describing how he did his amazing tricks. Although modern escape artists know how he arranged his amazing deeds, none of them has been able to perform in the same way.

Questions and Discussion

1. Since Harry Houdini's acts were **controversial**, people often expressed differing opinions about them. Mark statements below that are opinions with an O. Leave the others blank.

    _____ a. Houdini gave exhibitions.

    _____ b. Houdini was a great showman.

    _____ c. Houdini should not have left notes that told how he did his acts.

    _____ d. Houdini wasted his life. He should have gotten a regular job.

    _____ e. Houdini was very strong.

2. Let's assume that you are writing a story about the United States. Which of the statements below would be opinions and which would be statements of fact? Write fact or opinion in the blanks.

    _____ a. The population of the country is growing.

    _____ b. We are beginning to have too many people.

    _____ c. There are both large cities and small towns.

    _____ d. City life is more interesting.

    _____ e. We have millions of miles of road.

    _____ f. People are driving much too fast.

    _____ g. Sports are often featured in news articles.

    _____ h. Athletes get more attention than they deserve.

3. People will always make both statements of fact and statements of opinion. Explain what you believe is the importance of each.

    a. Expressing opinions is important because

    _____

    _____

    b. Providing facts is important because

    _____

    _____

DISTINGUISHING BETWEEN FACT AND OPINIONS

A Home Away From Home

Words you'll need to know...
settlers people who move in to live in a new area

Have you ever thought about how your life would change if you were to suddenly move from the United States to China or Africa and join another family–a family with very different habits and customs? You would probably be frightened and confused, at least for a while.

As strange as it may seem, this is exactly what happened to a little girl named Frances Slocum, who lived the first five years of her life in eastern Pennsylvania. One day when she was outside playing, three Delaware Indians captured her and took her to what is now the state of Indiana. For nearly 60 years her family knew nothing about what had become of her.

The Native Americans who adopted Slocum were good to her. She quickly learned their ways and they named her Maconaqua, or Little Bear Woman. Slocum married a Delaware Indian, then later a Miami brave. Like most of the Indians with whom she lived, Slocum learned to fear the **settlers**. She did not think of them as her friends and family because she could scarcely remember her former life.

Finally in 1835, over 57 years after she had been captured, Slocum was discovered by a trader, George Ewing. He told other traders of seeing a white woman living with the Indians in a log cabin along the banks of the Mississinewa River. Slocum talked with George Ewing in the Miami Indian language, and she agreed to meet with her brothers and sister. However, she did not want to leave her Indian friends to return to her family.

Questions and Discussion

1. See if you can mark the statements below as facts or opinions.

   _____ a. Frances Slocum was a brave girl.

   _____ b. Slocum lived with the Indians.

   _____ c. Her family did not know where she was.

   _____ d. Slocum lived in a log cabin.

   _____ e. Slocum did not want to return to her family.

   _____ f. Slocum lived five years in Pennsylvania.

   _____ g. Slocum should have returned home.

2. Write the fact from the article that seems most unusual to you.

UNIT 2
Drawing Valid CONCLUSIONS

We draw conclusions–judgments or decisions made as a result of careful thought–about many objects, people, and events every day. We decide that we like some things we see and dislike others. Frequently, we jump to conclusions too quickly. Most of us have had to change our ideas about our classmates, our teachers, and even our friends. Our first impressions were often faulty because we had only limited experiences with these new friends. It is wiser to observe people over a period of time in a wide variety of situations before we draw definite conclusions about them.

Accurate conclusions are based on a careful examination of all the facts in a situation as well as thoughtful reasoning. When a young girl saw that a tent was being erected in her village she thought that a circus was coming to town. She didn't know that the tent might be used for a religious meeting, a car show, or a political rally.

When Carol Ramirez visited Puerto Rico during the summer she got sunburned and the hot pavements scorched her feet. She concluded that the only reason people stayed on the island was because they couldn't afford to leave. Carol did not realize that during the fall, winter, and spring seasons Puerto Rico is very pleasant.

When Jimmy Roberts saw that his new neighbors had a huge dog he concluded that they were afraid of robbers. He didn't realize that the dog might be used in dog shows or by members of the family for hunting.

In drawing conclusions we must also be careful about the words we use. Words such as *nobody, everyone, always, never, all, no one,* and *none* can make our conclusions incorrect. If you conclude that everyone at school loves sports, you are probably wrong. If you state that nobody can get a good grade from Mrs. Roberts, that conclusion is probably also false.

Which conclusions below are probably false? Put a check beside them.

_____ Everyone cheats sometimes.

_____ The use of drugs contributes to crime.

_____ You can never take a trip without some kind of problems.

_____ Everyone enjoys a good dish of ice cream.

Read the article about Ernest Shackleton and check the answers that represent the best conclusions.

Shackleton's Trials

Words you'll need to know...
expedition group trip over large distances
whaling village port from which ships sail to hunt whales

Sir Ernest Shackleton dreamed of being the first person to reach the South Pole. He had come within 97 miles of his goal in 1907. This was almost four years before Ronald Amundsen reached the South Pole. Blinding storms and a shortage of food forced Shackleton to quit.

In 1914 Shackleton led another **expedition** to the South Pole. His ship, the *Endurance*, reached the polar regions. The huge mountains of ice made the journey impossible. The ship was soon crushed by the ice. This was a heavy blow to the men who were fighting desperately for their lives.

Shackleton and his men were forced to set out in the small boats that they had taken from the sinking ship. The tiny lifeboats offered little shelter from the fierce winds. After many freezing days and nights, the crew finally landed on Elephant Island. They were the first humans ever to reach that shore. Since the island offered no food or shelter, Shackleton decided to push onward.

The group tried next for South Georgia. It was 800 miles to the north. They knew that there was a small whaling village there. Six men left in the largest of their boats. They took turns steering, and then they bundled up in their frozen sleeping bags. The winds and sea were relentless. Frigid ocean spray pounded the boat constantly.

On their fourteenth day at sea Shackleton sighted land. Soon the boat was beached in a small cove. The men staggered ashore. They had landed on the uninhabited side of the island! Shackleton and his men climbed for two days and nights over icy mountains. At times they were nearly blown off the peaks. They suffered cold and frostbite. Finally, they struggled into the little **whaling village**. Their ordeal was over!

Questions and Discussion

Decide which conclusion is most likely based on what you have read. Circle the letter of the best answer.

1. What would have happened if Shackleton had not set out for South Georgia?

    a. The crew would have perished.

    b. The crew would have been rescued.

2. What would have happened if Shackleton and his crew had not been physically strong and brave?

    a. They would have gotten through despite their weaknesses.

    b. They would have given up almost immediately.

The firefly and Indian rope trick reports require you to write out or explain your conclusions at the end.

Fireflies for Sale

Words you'll need to know...
chemicals tiny parts or elements that form liquids, gases, or solid objects
pupae insects inside cocoons
reproduce give birth

The members of the Sigma Firefly Scientists Club made $40,000 in one year collecting fireflies. The club was started in 1972 in St. Louis. It has thousands of members in over twenty-five states. Members collect millions of fireflies each year. They receive a few cents for each one they sell.

The Sigma Chemical Company uses the fireflies to get rare chemicals they need in their business. These chemicals are used for special studies, including cancer research.

These insects are called fireflies, lightning bugs, or lightning beetles. They begin life as eggs. Often the eggs themselves give off light. They change into worms for two years or more. Then they develop into pupae. In 10 days the pupa becomes an adult. It lives only a few days or weeks.

The firefly's light is of great interest to scientists. Five chemicals are responsible for this light. Two of the chemicals are useful in detecting the presence of living organisms. These are the chemicals scientists use in cancer research. Besides cancer research, the chemicals are also being used by NASA to search for life in outer space.

Although there is no lack of fireflies, not enough of them have been caught to meet the need. They cannot be raised in a lab because they do not reproduce in captivity. They must be caught. Usually, groups work together in collecting the little beetles. However, one man from Iowa, working alone, made $4,671 in 1995!

In this article you have learned the following facts about fireflies:
- The Sigma Chemical Company is willing to pay money for each firefly it receives.
- Fireflies contain chemicals that are useful in scientific research.
- One man from Iowa made $4,671 by catching fireflies.

Here are some additional facts about fireflies not given in the story.
- People in tropical countries sometimes put large numbers of fireflies in jars and use them as lanterns.
- People traveling through dense jungle areas at night sometimes attach fireflies to their shoes to light the forest floor in front of them.

Questions and Discussion

1. What conclusion can you come to about the firefly based on the above facts? Circle the correct letter.

    a. Fireflies are in danger of dying out.

    b. Fireflies are fun to catch.

    c. Fireflies are valuable insects.

2. Write your own conclusion about the usefulness of fireflies in other countries.

The Indian Rope Trick

Words you'll need to know...
hoax something that is fake, not true
hypnotized put in a trance

Have you ever heard of the Indian rope trick? It is a trick that was supposedly perfected in India. People who claim to have seen it say that a magician throws a rope into the air. The rope seems to be pulled up into the clouds. A small boy or girl then climbs the rope and disappears. When the rope is pulled back down, the child appears again.

Many people believe that the public is being fooled. Some doubt that the trick has ever even been done. When King George and Queen Mary of Great Britain toured India no one could find a magician willing to perform the trick. Even one of the wealthiest Indian princesses could not persuade any magicians to try the trick.

A group of scientists from London has also studied the reports of Indian rope trick. They concluded that there was no evidence, anywhere on Earth, of such a trick being successfully performed. The scientists offered $2,500 to anyone who would demonstrate the trick. No one has ever tried to win the money.

People suggest that witnesses who claim to have seen the trick have been **hypnotized** by the magician. The rope does not climb into the air but the witnesses are led to believe that this is happening.

Questions and Discussion

1. Decide which of the following statements is the best conclusion based on what you have read. Circle the letter.

    a. People are not interested in the rope trick.

    b. Hindu fakirs know how to do the trick.

    c. The Indian rope trick is a **hoax**.

    d. Witnesses have not said they actually have seen the trick done.

2. In the space below, tell why the conclusion you chose is best.

    _____
    _____
    _____

See if you can write out your own conclusions for the next two descriptions of famous people.

The Knife-Swallowing Incident

> **Words you'll need to know...**
> **astonished** filled with sudden wonder
> **gestures** hand signals
> **shunned** avoided
> **trail blazer** person who opens new trails

Daniel Boone was the greatest **trail blazer** and woodsman of his day. He explored thousands of miles of forests. He built trails into vast regions of Kentucky. The Wilderness Road was his most famous route.

Daniel was raised in a large Quaker family in Pennsylvania. His family **shunned** fighting

and bloodshed. Although Daniel was no coward he avoided killing whenever possible. He often used quick thinking and quiet ways in place of brute force. Daniel's knowledge of the frontier and people saved his life on several occasions.

Once, when Daniel Boone was eating with some friends in the woods a large group of men appeared. The men were wild-looking but seemed friendly. Boone pretended not to notice the men, but he quietly told his friends to be prepared. He then walked over to the men.

Boone made a few friendly **gestures** and then asked to look at a man's knife. The man with the knife was hesitant but finally gave it to Boone. Daniel quickly opened his mouth and pretended to swallow the weapon. Actually, he slipped it up his sleeve. The men were surprised by Boone's trick. They were even more amazed when Boone said the knife tasted good.

Soon Boone made some more movements with his hands. He appeared to draw the knife back out of his mouth. He returned the weapon to its owner and went back to his own small group of friends.

The wild-looking men soon left. They were **astonished** to see a man who could swallow knives.

20 DRAWING VALID CONCLUSIONS

Questions and Discussion

1. From this report, what can you conclude about Daniel Boone's interest in adventure?

   _____
   _____
   _____
   _____
   _____

2. What can you conclude about Daniel Boone's relationship with people?

   _____
   _____
   _____
   _____
   _____

3. What can you conclude about Daniel Boone's intelligence?

   _____
   _____
   _____
   _____
   _____

4. What can you conclude about the reasons why the wild men left Daniel Boone and his friends?

   _____
   _____
   _____
   _____
   _____
   _____
   _____

Cheiro the Great

Words you'll need to know...
client customer
palm prints the shape of a hand made in ink
Scotland Yard the main police station in England

The officers of **Scotland Yard** knew the victim had been killed, but they knew little else. They had investigated every detail of the crime scene, but their search for the criminal had gotten them nowhere.

The Scotland Yard men were preparing to leave the crime scene. At that moment, a well-dressed man appeared at the door, "May I help?" he asked.

The police officers were not expecting any help, but they felt they could certainly use some assistance.

The young man examined the bloody handprints on the wall. "The criminal is a young man," he said. "He is well-to-do and carries a gold watch in a front trouser pocket. He is a near relative of the unfortunate victim."

The detectives asked the visitor to identify himself. "I'm Cheiro the Great!" he told them as he handed them his business card.

In just twenty-four hours, the police had captured the murderer. He was young and wealthy and he carried a gold watch in his front trouser pocket. He was the murdered man's son.

Cheiro became famous all over London. In 1893 he left for New York. There he helped solve other complicated crimes. He was written up in the newspapers. A young woman who read about his feats asked if she could test his skills. He agreed.

The test was made up of **palm prints** of 13 well-known men. Only three judges knew the identity of the prints. Cheiro picked up one print after another and described the person to whom each print belonged. He scored perfectly on the test.

The newspapers heard of Cheiro's feats and praised him. Soon his fame spread around the world. He toured Europe. There he predicted that Czar Nicholas of Russia would lose everything, including his life, in 1917. This prediction came true.

In 1906 Cheiro's unusual powers deserted him, and he was charged with mishandling a **client**'s money. For this crime he spent 13 months in jail. In 1936, he died in a fall from a hotel window in Hollywood.

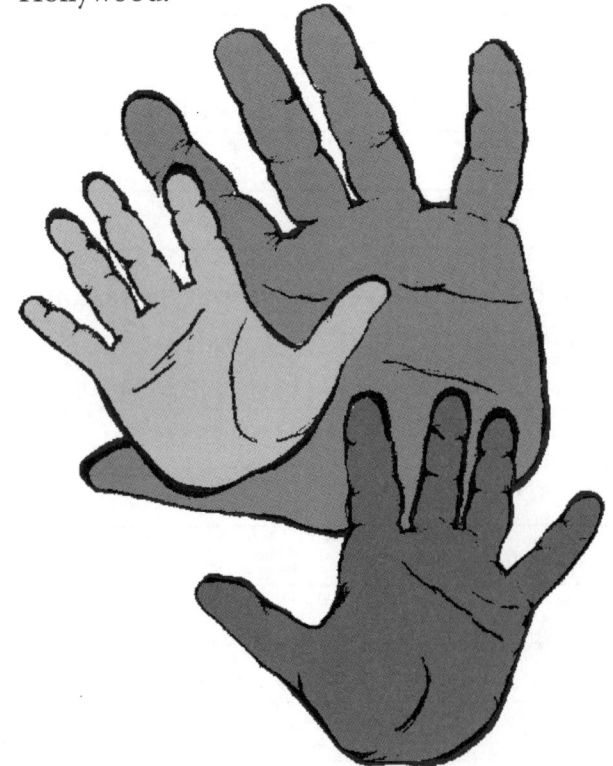

Questions and Discussion

1. From reading this article, what can you conclude about Cheiro's view of himself?

   _____
   _____
   _____
   _____
   _____

2. What can you conclude about other people's views of Cheiro?

   _____
   _____
   _____
   _____
   _____

3. What kind of conclusion can you make about Cheiro's special gifts?

   _____
   _____
   _____
   _____
   _____

4. After reading this brief description of Cheiro's life, what do you conclude about his honesty?

   _____
   _____
   _____
   _____
   _____
   _____
   _____

Using Magic Rods

Words you'll need to know...

dowser person who uses metal rods or sticks to find water

magnetic field an area where steel may be affected

When farmers or townspeople want to drill a well to get water, they sometimes call a dowser, or water witch, to help them find the best place to dig their well. The **dowser** uses a forked stick, rods, or a coat hanger to find out where the water is located beneath the surface of the ground. As the dowser walks, the forked stick or coat hanger usually dips down suddenly. This movement indicates the presence of water below.

Some people believe very strongly in the value of water witching. They point out that Evelyn Penrose of England has been 80% accurate in her attempts to find not only water but also metals and oil. Believers feel that water witching works because of **magnetic fields** along the Earth's surface. Water beneath the surface often causes changes in the magnetic fields. These changes, in turn, cause the dowser's stick to move. Geologists, however, point out that changes in the Earth's magnetic field may be caused by many different conditions besides water.

People who do not believe in water witching think that the whole thing is a hoax. They point out that water exists beneath much of the Earth's surface and that any person who is a clever guesser can be correct much of the time. An observant water witch may study the way the land is formed and notice where plants are growing most abundantly. This, according to doubters, may give him or her more clues than a forked stick.

Questions and Discussion

1. Some scientists who study water sources (hydrologists) believe that underground water and other materials are more quickly found by modern instruments. Which would you use and why?

   _____
   _____
   _____

2. If a farmer pays a dowser to find water, what can you conclude about the farmer's beliefs?

   _____
   _____
   _____

The Discoverer of America

Words you'll need to know...

New England northeastern part of the United States

impressions a person's viewpoint about something

Manjiro Nakahama (MAHN jiroh NAH kah hah mah) was a remarkable man! In 1841 he set sail from Japan with four friends. They planned to fish for a short time and then return. Shortly after they reached the open sea, a huge storm came up. It blew them to a small reef in the Pacific known as Hurricane Island. There was little to eat on the island. After six months of near-starvation, they were picked up by an American whaling ship. The whaling ship took them to Hawaii.

Four of the seamen stayed in Hawaii, but Manjiro went on to **New England**. There he learned the whaling trade and studied English. Although Manjiro was content, he was also homesick for Japan. He finally worked his way to the West Coast of the United States. By saving money, he was able to buy passage to Hawaii and then to Japan.

Manjiro knew that he would likely be killed when he returned to Japan. For many centuries Japan had been a country cut off from the rest of the world. Few outsiders were allowed in, and the Japanese who left were forbidden to return. The Japanese, however, were so fascinated with Manjiro's tales of America that they decided not to kill him.

Manjiro became an important person in Japan. His fellow Japanese were so curious about his **impressions** of American life that they provided him with artists who drew pictures of American tools, furniture, musical instruments, and buildings according to Manjiro's descriptions. In a drawing they made of the Old North Church, a Boston landmark, the building looked more like a pagoda than a church. Manjiro is remembered in Japan to this day as "the discoverer of America."

Questions and Discussion

1. The Japanese were cut off from the rest of the world because of a conclusion they made about all foreigners. Which of the following statements do you suppose contains that conclusion? Circle the correct letter.

    a. They concluded that foreigners would invade and conquer Japan.

    b. They concluded that foreigners were kind people who wished to be left alone.

    c. They concluded that foreigners would introduce new and interesting customs.

    d. They concluded that foreigners would have trouble reaching Japan.

2. Japan's conclusion about foreigners was based on some experiences they had in dealing with outsiders during the 1600's. Do you suppose those experiences were good or bad? Why?

A Prisoner and a Shoemaker

Words you'll need to know...
carnival festival or street party
erupted blew up, exploded
looters people who steal things

On May 8, 1902, Mt. Pelee on Martinique in the West Indies **erupted**. The volcano destroyed the entire town of St. Pierre and killed 38,000 people.

Mt. Pelee had been giving warnings for weeks before the explosion. But for some reason, no one believed anything serious would happen. Then, all at once, the end came. Scalding steam, deadly gases, and volcanic dust killed everything and everyone in sight, with two exceptions. Two people, a prisoner and a shoemaker, escaped and lived to tell about the disaster.

The prisoner, a man named Ceparis, was locked in an underground jail. Charged with murder, he expected to live out his life in prison.

As Ceparis waited for his breakfast on the morning of May 8 the sky became dark. Hot air filled with ashes flooded his cell. Even though he quickly turned away from the window, his back and legs were burned with the heat of the ash. For three days he remained in his cell, protected by its location and thick walls. Finally, outside help arrived and he was rescued.

Ceparis was pardoned after his recovery. He later worked in circuses and **carnivals**. He was called "The Prisoner of St. Pierre." As part of his act, he locked himself in a cell like the one in St. Pierre. He died in 1929.

The other survivor, Leandre, a shoemaker, was sitting on the doorstep of his house when the volcano erupted. People all around him were dying. With his legs bleeding, Leandre ran from his burning house to the next town, 3.6 miles east of St. Pierre.

Leandre was found and taken to a hospital. He later returned to St. Pierre as part of a special police force that guarded the town against **looters**. He lived until 1936.

Questions and Discussion

1. What conclusion did the people of St. Pierre make about Mt. Pelee? Circle the letter of the correct answer.

    a. They concluded they would all die if the volcano erupted.

    b. They concluded the volcano was harmless.

    c. They concluded they deserved whatever they got.

    d. They concluded the eruption had already taken place.

2. The townspeoples' conclusion about Mt. Pelee was probably based on their previous experience with volcanoes. What do you suppose that experience was?

UNIT 3
Classifying
OBJECTS, PEOPLE AND EVENTS

> **Words you'll need to know...**
> **characteristics** features or nature
> **classify** place in categories
> **utensils** household tools

Sometime during your elementary school years a teacher probably emptied a box containing many different kinds of items on a table. There were scraps of cloth, buttons, rocks, pencils, coins, tiny toys, pieces of string, wire, etc. She then challenged you and your classmates to group the items according to a plan you figured out or designed. The rest of the kids were then supposed to guess what system or plan you were using to group the items.

In those early years of school you almost always grouped objects according to their physical **characteristics**. You would sort them so the round pieces were together or, perhaps, you put all the red items in a group. In addition, some students might arrange them according to size.

Later, when you reached the upper grades you began grouping things according to their uses—all these **utensils** are used in cooking. These tools don't look alike, but they are all used by carpenters. This is much harder. You can't just look at them. You have to know something about them. Cars, trains, and boats don't look alike. You have to know that they are all used for transporting people and materials. You can, therefore, **classify** them as transportation.

We can also classify things according to the way they react to their surroundings. Some materials will float on water; others will sink. Some animals eat meat; others eat only plants. Some vegetables, like lettuce, grow on top of the ground; others, like beets, grow under the ground. We can depend on these things in nature to act (behave) in this way. Therefore, we can classify them according to these characteristics.

See if you can match one of the ways we classify things shown in the box with each of the situations listed below the box.

> **classified according to <u>similar physical characteristics</u>**
>
> **classified because they <u>have the same uses</u>**
>
> **classified according to how they <u>react to surroundings</u>**

The first three are done for you.

react to surroundings	1. These trees drop their leaves in winter.
similar physical characteristics	2. These flowers are all red.
have the same uses	3. These soaps are all used for washing walls.
_____	4. These animals all migrate.
_____	5. These pillows are all soft.
_____	6. These are all painting supplies.
_____	7. These are very strong boards.
_____	8. These gloves are for gardening.
_____	9. These balloons lost air quickly.
_____	10. These planes can carry more passengers.

There are so many kinds of living and non-living things in the world that we can't possibly keep track of them all. By grouping them into classifications (rocks, insects, forms of energy, buildings, types of transportation, forms of music, etc.), we can understand much more quickly what a person is talking about.

Many of the directories we use are organized around classifications. Newspapers have classified ads for cars, pets, household goods, job openings, repairmen, etc. These notices are usually found near the back of the paper. They are sometimes called "want-ads."

Telephone directories also list thousands of sources of goods and services. If you don't know who to call for roofing, car repair, child care, building supplies, insurance, or printing, you will find places to call in the Yellow Pages. This is much, much easier than calling friends for suggestions.

One of the largest classification systems can be found on the Internet. People seeking information can type in key words to start their search. They may also consult a server, like Yahoo, and examine the categories they offer. This vast body of information is growing constantly.

Odd Habits of Bees

Words you'll need to know...
cobbler a person who mends shoes and boots
floral related to flowers

Sam Rogers was a **cobbler** and part-time mail carrier who kept bees most of his life. When Sam died in 1924 there were many people at the funeral. As the people arrived at the cemetery, they were amazed. Old Sam's bees were coming to the funeral and they were there by the thousands.

The Reverend John Ayling reported to news people, "It was a fantastic thing. As far as we could see, there was a line of bees. They came straight from Sam's beehives a mile away. The bees streamed into the cemetery and to the place of burial. The graveside services were held with the heavy buzzing of bees. As soon as the services were over the bees flew away."

In 1956, another beekeeper, John Zepka, died in Adams, Massachusetts. He had raised bees all his life too. He loved to work with them and care for them.

When the funeral reached the cemetery, the bees were already there. Thousands hung from the frame of the tent over the grave and many more were on the **floral** pieces. During the graveside services they were quiet. When the services were over, the bees left. They buzzed loudly as they made a beeline back to the farm.

Questions and Discussion

1. Bees are obviously different from pets. If we set up two classifications, it is possible to see the differences. List the phrases below to show the differences.

They like to be played with	Sometimes follow strangers
Will not fight with others of their kind	Enjoy human companionship
Must stay outdoors	Must be provided with food
Make their own food	May join in groups of thousands

Bees

_____

_____

_____

_____

Pets

_____

_____

_____

_____

2. In this exercise, it is possible to see how items or facilities can be grouped under more than one heading. There are 17 words listed and 38 blanks. Obviously, some words will be used twice.

campfire	hotel	letter jacket
hiking boots	fishing pole	dining room
restaurant	bathing suit	sleeping bag
tent	wading boots	ski
cafeteria	ski boots	cabin
diner	motel	

Sports Items

_____
_____
_____
_____
_____
_____

Places to Sleep

_____
_____
_____
_____
_____
_____

Buildings

_____
_____
_____
_____
_____
_____

Outdoor Equipment

_____
_____
_____
_____
_____
_____

Clothing

_____
_____
_____
_____
_____
_____

Places to Eat

_____
_____
_____
_____
_____
_____

Swallowed by a Whale

Words you'll need to know...
delirious out of your mind
ordeal stressful test

About 150 years ago James Bartley worked on a whaling ship in the North Atlantic Ocean. At that time sailors chased whales in longboats. These were rowboats that they lowered from the decks of the large sailing ships. As the men approached the whales they would throw a large spear (harpoon) with a rope attached.

On one occasion, a whale turned and attacked the longboat in which Bartley was seated. There was a tremendous crash. The longboat was smashed. Another boat picked up the men from the water but they could not find Bartley.

Shortly before sunset the whale floated to the surface. It was dead. The crew attached a cable to the body and brought the whale on board. Late that night, the crew removed the whale's stomach. They were amazed to see movement. The ship's doctor was called in to cut the stomach open. Out slid James Bartley! He was alive! He was a greenish color and unconscious. The crew immediately drenched him with sea water.

For several weeks Bartley lay unconscious in a cabin. He was tied up so he could not injure himself. During this time he was **delirious**. Gradually his mind cleared. A month passed before he could explain what had happened.

"I saw a huge mouth open, and I screamed. There were sharp pains as I was swept across the whale's teeth. All of a sudden I could feel myself sliding feet first down a slimy tube. I could breathe, but the heat and strong fishy smell made me pass out."

Bartley was in the whale's stomach for 15 hours. During this time, the acids that surrounded him took their toll. He lost all the hair on his body and his eyes became weak.

After the accident, Bartley decided to leave the sea forever. He became a shoemaker. He was examined by doctors several times. He lived for 18 years following his **ordeal**. On his tomb are these words: "A Modern Jonah."

James Bartley did not plan his ordeal. Some people, however, plan and perform acts that are equally incredible.

Questions and Discussion

1. Use two classifications: (a) Acts that can really be done and (b) Acts that must involve special illusions. How would you classify the following acts?

   > Putting a flaming torch in your mouth
   > Making an elephant disappear
   > Picking up a 400-pound weight
   > Disappearing from the stage and appearing in the back of the hall

   Acts that can really be done   Acts that must involve illusion

   _____   _____

   _____   _____

   _____   _____

   _____   _____

2. Read the three words in each lettered row. Decide why these words are in a group. Then find a word in the boxed list to add to each category.

   > nephew   salamander   shirt   after   barn   cheek
   > car   bush   porch   flute   plum   grin

a. lizard	spider	toad	_____
b. aunt	niece	uncle	_____
c. cabbage	egg	lemons	_____
d. now	before	later	_____
e. neck	tongue	eyes	_____
f. giggle	smile	laugh	_____
g. stable	shed	garage	_____
h. grass	flower	tree	_____
i. window	roof	door	_____
j. piano	violin	clarinet	_____
k. sweater	jacket	slacks	_____
l. truck	bus	motorcycle	_____

3. As was mentioned earlier, most things are part of larger groupings. Use the word lists to fill in the blanks below. List #1 should be used to fill in the left set of blanks.

	List 1		**List 2**	
	circus	plane	room	tree
	shoe	fruit	food	clothing
	sentences	door	stories	transportation
	branch	room	building	entertainment

a. A sandal is a kind of _____, which is part of our _____.

b. A peach is a kind of _____, which is a type of _____.

c. A knob is a part of a _____, which is part of a _____.

d. Words are parts of _____, which make up _____.

e. A leaf is part of a _____, which is found on a _____.

f. A door is part of a _____, which is part of a _____.

g. A wing is part of a _____, which is a kind of _____

h. A clown is in a _____, which is a kind of _____.

The Will to Succeed

Words you'll need to know...
navigation steering a ship
plaque large decorative plate
provisions supplies of food and clothing
sledge a giant sled

You have probably had friends who simply had to succeed. They wanted to win the music contest or get to be captain of the tennis team. You saw them practicing, always practicing! Their parents worried that, after all that practice, they would be terribly disappointed if they fell short of their dreams.

Matthew Henson (1867-1955), an African-American boy from Maryland, had this kind of overpowering drive to succeed. He wanted to learn about life. He wanted to achieve things but he got no help from his family. His stepmother, Nellie, beat him and almost starved him to death. Henson was so frightened and miserable that he packed his things and escaped in the middle of winter. He had no shoes and just a light cotton jacket. He cut his blanket into squares, folded them, and wrapped them around his feet. He wasn't sure where he was going but he knew he couldn't survive any longer in Nellie's house.

Matt was so hungry that he begged for food the next morning near a farm house. Fortunately, Janey Moore, an African-American woman, took him in. Matt did all kinds of jobs for Janey Moore. She paid him a dollar and a half a week for his help. Matt put the money under his mattress. After Matt had worked for Mrs. Moore for two years, he decided to try to get a job on a ship.

Matt walked to Baltimore where he met Captain Childs, skipper of the *Katie Hines*. Capt. Childs told Matt he could be his cabin boy. Matt dreamed of finding treasure. He found something much more valuable. Over the next five years, Capt. Childs taught Matt to read and write. He taught him geography, history, mathematics, and **navigation**. Capt. Childs talked about great historical figures as though they were his friends.

Matt got to see much of the world. One winter the *Katie Hines* was frozen in a Russian port. For four months the crew was entertained by Russian sailors and peasants. They took them on wolf hunts, which were followed by singing, dancing, and drinking late into the night.

Unfortunately, in 1883 on a voyage to Jamaica Captain Childs became violently ill. He died and the crew buried him at sea. Matt returned to shore to look for work. He found a poor job at a hat store, but it was there that he met Robert Perry, a naval officer, who desperately wanted to travel to the North Pole.

Perry invited Matt to join him in his explorations. They explored the arctic regions together for many years (1885-1909). At first, the team explored the Greenland ice cap. In 1885, the expedition overloaded their sledges. They were far too heavy to move up the ice caps. In 1898, the explorers had to turn back again because Perry's toes froze. In 1905, they came within 175 miles of the North Pole. In 1909, they finally reached the top of the world and Matt was given the honor of planting the American flag at the North Pole.

Perry and Henson were honored all over the world for their extraordinary achievements. Perry could never have succeeded, however, without Matt Henson. Matt was thoroughly acquainted with the life, customs, and language of the Eskimos. He built the sledges, he prepared the maps and **provisions**, he hunted the wild game, he built cooking stoves, and he saved the lives of several men on the expeditions.

Matt Henson lived until 1955. Upon his death, a bronze **plaque** was placed in the State House in Annapolis, Maryland, to honor his tremendous achievements and his life.

Questions and Discussion

1. We can classify Matt's achievements under at least three classifications:

    a. Planning—name one thing he planned.

    _____

    b. Building—name one thing he built.

    _____

    c. Communication—name a type of communication he mastered.

    _____

2. As you know, we can classify various types of books. See if you can list the titles of the books beneath the correct classifications.

    Titles of books:

    Lives of Famous Writers   *Three Magic Stories*
    Fairy Tales of China   *Trees and Plants*
    The Boyhood of Thomas Edison   *Geography of Europe*

    Fiction   Nonfiction   Biography

    _____   _____   _____

    _____   _____   _____

    _____   _____   _____

3. Some things are found under the ground and other things are found above the ground. Put the names under the correct classification headings. Choose words from the list.

potato	corn	oats	onion
sheep	limestone	peanuts	fox

    Above the ground   Under the ground

    _____   _____

    _____   _____

    _____   _____

    _____   _____

CLASSIFYING OBJECTS, PEOPLE, AND EVENTS   35

An Army of Animals

From 1810 to 1814 Bernardo O'Higgins and his Chilean soldiers were trying to free Chile from Spanish rule. They had few arms or other supplies.

The Spanish king sent many boatloads of soldiers to defeat O'Higgins's army. These Spanish soldiers had a hard time. The Chileans fought with courage and skill.

Finally, the king's soldiers surrounded the Chileans. They were trapped. O'Higgins thought up a plan. He asked his soldiers to round up all the mules, cows, sheep, and dogs they could find.

The animals were gathered, O'Higgins got on his horse, and he charged ahead. The frightened animals began to run. They became a stampeding, bellowing mass. The Spanish had never seen such a sight! They were very confused. They retreated as the animals rushed forward.

As the Spanish stood helplessly, the Chileans escaped by charging through the gap left by the animals. They were soon safe in the mountains. O'Higgins had won a crucial battle with an army of animals.

Three years later O'Higgins returned with four thousand soldiers. In 1818, he proclaimed Chile's independence.

Questions and Discussion

1. Most military leaders use weapons. There are a number of weapons listed. Classify them as old weapons or modern weapons.

armored tanks	**wooden battleships**	**spears**	**jet planes**
swords	**submarines**	**bombs**	**daggers**

   Old Weapons   Modern Weapons

   _____   _____

   _____   _____

   _____   _____

   _____   _____

   _____   _____

   _____   _____

2. We often classify items from very specific to very general. For example: Puff is a specific pet. She is part of a group called cats. Cats, in turn, are part of a larger group called mammals. Mammals belong to still a larger group called animals. The list would be marked as follows:

         __1__ animals

         __2__ mammals

         __3__ Puff

         __4__ cats

   For each group below, number the items from one to four. Use 1 for the most general object or idea. The most specific will be number 4.

   a. encyclopedia _____
      printed material _____
      book _____
      reference book _____

   b. boys _____
      Charles _____
      children _____
      people _____

   c. television _____
      Saturday Night Live _____
      comedy show _____
      entertainment _____

   d. Polly _____
      bird _____
      parrot _____
      pet _____

   e. shoes _____
      clothing _____
      sneakers _____
      footwear _____

   f. jet _____
      aircraft _____
      vehicle _____
      airplane _____

Do Animals Predict Atmospheric Changes?

Words you'll need to know...
atmosphere air surrounding the Earth
examined watched carefully

For many years scientists have been observing various animals. They want to see if changes in their behavior can be used to predict the coming of earthquakes, cold winters, or storms. In this country we have observed woolly worms and groundhogs. In Japan, scientists have **examined** catfish before and after earthquakes. So far, these experts have had difficulty predicting disasters or climatic changes by watching animal behavior. However, one recent experiment with oysters does serve to remind us that creatures can sometimes sense very slight changes in the atmosphere.

Oysters are sea creatures that resemble clams. They live on the bottoms of bays near the ocean. Oysters don't move about much but they can open and close their shells. They live together in large groups called oyster beds. When the oysters are ready to be harvested they are scraped from the bays with large rakes.

Over the years scientists have noticed that oysters open and close their shells with the coming and going of the tides. Scientists wondered what the oysters would do if there were no tides. They decided to transport several hundred oysters in dark, sealed tanks 360 miles inland. At first, the oysters continued to follow their normal rhythm, opening and closing according to the tides on their home beaches.

After 15 days a very strange thing happened. Their opening and closing rhythms changed to what they would be if the sea's tides were washing the shores of their new homes. The shellfish opened when the moon–which controls the tides–was directly over their new home. Since the oysters were in completely darkened tanks and kept at a constant temperature, the scientists knew that neither light nor changes in temperature were causing them to open and close.

The scientists who conducted the experiments have not been able to explain exactly what caused the oysters to change their patterns. They think that the oysters might have been reacting to the slight gravitational pull of the moon even when there was no light or tide to influence them.

Questions and Discussion

1. We often call animals shellfish, but we know they are not fish. Arrange the names in the box under two classifications to show the difference between fish and other sea creatures.

| turtles | crabs | bass | tuna | oysters | sharks |

Creatures that are fish

1. _____

2. _____

3. _____

Creatures that are not fish

1. _____

2. _____

3. _____

2. Three of the items in the following groups can be classified together into a category. Cross off the two that don't fit and write the name of the category in the blank.

   a. slide   swing   bed pillow   monkey bars
   _____

   b. harmonica   cello   violin   trumpet   guitar
   _____

   c. waffles   oatmeal   toast   meatloaf   beets
   _____

   d. operating table   butter   surgeon   plumber   scalpel
   _____

   e. Mississippi   Atlantic   Nile   Pacific   Arctic
   _____

   f. razor blade   golf ball   pin   knife   bucket
   _____

   g. Dalmation   jaguar   beagle   poodle   owl
   _____

3. Try placing the words that are listed under the three category headings.

   | seeds   magazine   cook   hose   menus   librarian |
   | gardener   shovel   newspapers |

Occupations

_____

_____

_____

Things you can read

_____

_____

_____

Things in a hardware store

_____

_____

_____

CLASSIFYING OBJECTS, PEOPLE, AND EVENTS   39

A Prisoner in Parliament

Words you'll need to know...
bankruptcy   financial failure, broke

If an adult in this country does not repay a large loan he or she may have to declare **bankruptcy**. The court can then require the person to sell some belongings to pay some or all of the debt. Many years ago in England people who could not pay their debts were thrown into prison. They were not given their freedom until their debts were paid.

John Gully was in an English prison because he couldn't pay his debts. He had little hope for the future. He had no family or friends who could pay his debts.

Henry Pierce was the boxing champion in England at that time. He went to the prison to entertain the inmates. Gully was chosen to fight Pierce. To everyone's surprise, Gully won.

The news of what happened soon spread throughout England. A group of gamblers decided to pay Gully's debts. Gully got out of prison and began to box. He fought Henry Pierce again. He lost in the fifty-ninth round. After that, Gully won all his fights. In 1807, Pierce retired. Gully became the new heavyweight champion of England.

Gully quit boxing a little later. He bought racing horses. Two of his horses won the famous English Derby.

After that, Gully entered politics. In 1832 he was elected to the House of Commons. He served several terms in parliament. He died at the age of 90. He left a large fortune and a fine country estate. He had come a long way from his lonely days in prison.

Questions and Discussion

1. Boxing is clearly one of the most violent sports. It is possible to classify sports as violent and non-violent. Look at the sports listed and then classify them.

figure skating	ice hockey	volleyball	football
basketball	wrestling	bowling	running track

   Violent Sports   Nonviolent Sports

   _____   _____

   _____   _____

   _____   _____

   _____   _____

40   CLASSIFYING OBJECTS, PEOPLE, AND EVENTS

2. In this exercise, you are not given the classifications separately. They are mixed in with all the items. First, locate the headings, such as *dishware*. Then list the items below each heading.

sapphire	ruby	helicopter	ax
pliers	bowl	saucer	wrench
saw	hot-air-balloon	plates	jewels
plane	cup	jet	platter
screw driver	tools	dishware	aircraft
rocket	diamond	pearl	emerald

CLASSIFYING OBJECTS, PEOPLE, AND EVENTS 41

UNIT 4
Recognizing Sequences
IDENTIFYING STEPS IN A REPORT OR STORY

Have you ever asked a small child to tell you a story? If you have, you probably noticed that the events in the story were mixed up. There was probably no real beginning or ending.

As we get older, we pay a lot more attention to the order in which things take place. We don't normally bake a cake without following a recipe. We usually don't try to teach a game without reviewing the steps to be followed. We don't try to assemble furniture without first reading the directions.

A well-written story will normally consist of a clear set of events. A good report will also have very specific points. We expect writers to arrange their stories so that we can easily follow the happenings they are describing for us.

If you were reporting a fire, you might use the steps below:

Fire is discovered.
        Fire alarm is sounded.
                Firefighters arrive.
                      People are rescued.
                              Fire is put out.

Now see if you can arrange these events about a trip on similar steps.

1. riding on the highway
2. planning the trip
3. getting there
4. unpacking
5. packing
6. stopping for lunch

There are four short scientific reports on the next page. See if you can number the four steps in each report as they occurred.

42   RECOGNIZING SEQUENCES

Desert Shrimp

Although most shrimp come from the ocean, one little shrimp lives in desert water holes. When the mud dries up the shrimp almost stop living, but the shrimp come back to life when it finally rains.

Scientists have found these shrimp eggs in dried mudholes in the desert. When they soak the eggs in water they hatch into shrimp. Some of the eggs are 25 years old! That certainly is a long time to wait for a drink of water!

Number the events below from 1 to 4 as they occurred in the report.

_____ The shrimp eggs lay for many years without water.

_____ The eggs hatched into baby shrimp.

_____ Scientists soaked the shrimp eggs in a desert water hole.

_____ A female shrimp laid eggs in a desert water hole.

Bee Messages

Honeybees work very hard gathering nectar from flowers to make honey. To make one pound of honey the bees must travel about 43,000 miles and collect 30,000 tiny drops of nectar. Scientists recently discovered that bees that have found a good supply of nectar share the good news with other bees through a "honey dance." The dance tells the bees how far away and in what direction they can find nectar. Obviously, this method of communication makes gathering nectar a much easier and faster process.

Number the steps below to tell how honeybees cooperate in producing honey.

_____ The bees that find nectar return and do a honey dance to let the other bees know where the nectar is located.

_____ Bees from the entire hive go to where the nectar was found.

_____ The bees use the nectar they bring back to make honey.

_____ The bees search the region around their hive for nectar.

Animals with Egg Teeth

Animals born inside an egg are specially equipped with the means to break through the hard shell even though they are weak.

Most snakes and baby birds, for example, are hatched with a small, sharp, and very hard "egg tooth." This special tooth makes it possible for the little snake or bird to break the shell of the egg and escape. Within a few hours after hatching, the egg tooth falls off.

Number the events below from 1 to 4 as they occurred in the report.

_____ The egg tooth on the mouth of each newborn snake drops off.

_____ The adult female snake lays the egg.

_____ The tiny snake inside the egg gradually develops, and an egg tooth grows on the front of the tiny snake's mouth.

_____ The tiny snake uses its egg tooth to break the eggshell around him.

Water, Water Everywhere

Drinking a lot of ocean water can make you sick. For this reason, sailors who travel long distances have to carry their drinking water with them. Hundreds of years ago, sailors carried their water in barrels.

Modern sailors still can't drink water directly from the ocean, but ships today can make their own fresh water. Modern ships have machines that turn salt water into drinking water by using evaporation. Salt water is heated until the water turns to steam. The steam is collected and cooled. Cooling turns the steam into water that has no salt left in it. This water is good for drinking.

Number the steps below from 1 to 4 as they are used in making drinking water.

_____ Collect the steam that has come from the heated sea water.

_____ Collect the water that has come from the steam.

_____ Heat the sea water to a very hot temperature.

_____ Collect sea water from the ocean.

RECOGNIZING SEQUENCES

Here is a longer description. See if you can number the ten events as they occurred in the story.

Mary Lindley Murray

Words you'll need to know...
devised made up
historical marker sign and brief description to mark the place of an important event

Mary Murray lived near New York City during the Revolutionary War. General Howe and 8,000 British soldiers landed near her home and began their march. General George Washington decided to lead his small army out of the area to avoid possible capture. Knowing that General Howe's army would be coming her way, Murray **devised** a plan to give the Americans more time to get away. She sent her maid to the attic to watch the countryside for signs of Washington's army. "You can follow their progress by the dust their horses and wagons send into the air. Don't come downstairs until you are certain that General Washington has escaped."

While the maid watched carefully from the attic Murray prepared for the next part of her plan. As General Howe and his soldiers approached, she went out to greet them and offer them refreshments. After they had finished their cool drinks, Murray invited the General to dinner. He could not refuse her kind offer. It was getting late and dinner was nearly over when the maid appeared with a tray of cakes. Her smile told Murray that the plan had worked. General Washington and his army would live to fight another day.

Today in New York City a **historical marker** stands in memory of the bravery of Mary Murray and her maid.

Questions and Discussion

Number these sentences from 1 to 10 to show when things happened in the story.

_____ The maid brings dessert.

_____ Murray makes a plan.

_____ General Washington plans his retreat.

_____ Murray greets General Howe.

_____ Murray's maid goes to the attic.

_____ Murray serves refreshments.

_____ General Howe lands in New York.

_____ Murray knows the plan has worked.

_____ General Howe stays for dinner.

_____ General Washington escapes.

Now see if you can mark which events came before or after other events in the next two stories.

Nancy Hart

Nancy Hart lived with her husband and children near Augusta, Georgia, during the Revolutionary War. Hart did not like the British, and so she tried to help the Americans.

One day, Nancy Hart was working in the cabin when she heard a horse gallop up. When she saw that it was an American being chased by the British she allowed him to ride right through the front door, out the back door, and hide in the woods behind the cabin. When the British arrived they demanded food, but Hart said she didn't have any. A British soldier saw a turkey in the yard and shot it. "Now cook it for us," he demanded.

Hart sent her daughter to the spring to get water for the cooking pot. Hart hoped she would blow the conch shell hidden near the spring to call her husband and the men from the fields.

After Hart gave the British wine and they began to relax, she decided to steal their guns. She took some pine wedges out from between the logs in the cabin and quietly slipped the guns out through the hole. Only two guns were left when one of the soldiers noticed what she was doing. Hart quickly grabbed the last two guns and fired them one after the other into the air.

Just then, her daughter returned home from the spring and whispered, "Father is coming." A few minutes later, Benjamin Hart arrived with the other men.

Nancy Hart's courage and quick thinking saved the lives of several Americans. She was an important hero of the Revolutionary War.

Questions and Discussion

The sentences below have words in parentheses. Cross out one word in each pair to make the sentences correct.

1. A British soldier shot the turkey (before, after) the soldiers arrived at the cabin demanding something to eat.

2. Hart sent her daughter to the spring (before, after) the British demanded food.

3. Hart gave the British wine (before, after) she stole their guns.

4. Hart made a hole in the wall (before, after) she slipped the guns outside.

5. Hart's daughter returned to the cabin (before, after) Hart had fired the guns.

6. The men from the fields returned to the cabin (before, after) Hart's daughter arrived.

Nellie Bly

Words you'll need to know...
rickshaw a cart pulled by a man

Nellie Bly was a remarkable woman who became a newspaper reporter. For many years, she wrote about people who were mistreated. She first told about workers who worked under very bad conditions; then she wrote about slums where poor people were crowded together.

Later, Bly asked her editor to let her pretend she was mentally ill and allow her to be in a mental hospital. She saw that mentally sick people were treated badly. They were not fed well, they were beaten, and they were left alone for long periods of time. After Bly wrote about the bad conditions, treatment in mental hospitals improved.

Bly next pretended to steal from a store so she would be put in jail. When she saw that the prisoners were not treated well, she wrote about the shameful way men and women in prisons were beaten and neglected. Soon, prison conditions were also improved.

In 1889, Bly's editor let her travel around the world to try to beat the record time of 80 days set by Phineas Fogg. Bly went by train, ship, and **rickshaw**, and had an exciting trip! News reports told of her progress. She got back to New York in 72 days, six hours and 11 minutes. Through her travels and reporting, Bly captured the imaginations of her fellow Americans. She also helped many people who were badly treated.

Questions and Discussion

The sentences below have words in parentheses. Cross out one word in each pair to make the sentences correct.

1. Bly wrote about poor working conditions (before, after) she wrote about slums.

2. Bly wrote about prison conditions (before, after) she traveled around the world.

3. Bly saw that prisoners were mistreated (before, after) she stole from a store.

4. Bly wrote about prison conditions (before, after) she wrote about mental hospitals.

5. The treatment of mentally ill people changed (before, after) Bly wrote about the bad conditions.

6. A travel record was set by Phineas Fogg (before, after) Bly made her trip around the world.

In this next exercise, you will need to figure out and describe the sequences you find in this longer report.

Is Hypnosis a Trick?

Words you'll need to know...
allegedly supposedly
drowsy sleepy
perplexing puzzling, confusing
presumably probable, taken for granted
trance a dream-like feeling

When the hypnotist entered the auditorium at Fairview Middle School, the crowd became very quiet. Some in the audience were just curious to see how people would act under hypnosis. Others wanted to volunteer to be hypnotized themselves so they could see how it really felt. The hypnotist knew that he would be more successful with people who really wanted to be hypnotized so he called on those who seemed most eager to come up to the stage.

The hypnotist had the first student lie across three folding chairs. He held one finger in front of the student's eyes. He asked the student to focus her eyes only on his finger. He told the young woman that she was growing sleepy. He also told her that she was getting stronger. The lights were dimmed. A short time later, the hypnotist removed the middle chair. The girl's body remained suspended between the two remaining chairs. One chair supported her head and shoulders. The other chair supported her lower legs. The audience was amazed at the demonstration.

Although making a person strong and rigid may seem remarkable, it does not begin to compare with the astonishing claims of a Scottish doctor in India over 150 years ago. Dr. James Esdaile reportedly performed 73 painless surgical operations on natives of India while the patients were hypnotized. He even amputated damaged arms and legs on several occasions.

How Does Hypnosis Work?

You know that people daydream. While they are daydreaming, they seem to be unaware of things happening around them. They are in a kind of **trance**. The hypnotist tries to lead his patients into the same kind of trance. He starts by encouraging the subject (the person being treated) to ignore all thoughts and impressions except those he suggests. The hypnotist then asks the subject to focus his eyes on a particular object. As the patient focuses on the object, his eyes become tired and his mind becomes **drowsy**. The hypnotist then tells the patient that he will be able to hear and obey commands.

Next, the hypnotist tries a few simple commands to see if the patient is responding. The hypnotist may tell the subject that his left arm is so heavy that he can't lift it. If the patient is then told to lift his left arm and he cannot do it, the hypnotist knows that he is working with a subject who will respond to his commands. Only about half of all people can be hypnotized.

From this point on, the hypnotist gives the patient a series of statements or commands. The subject may be told that he will not feel pain when pricked by a pin. Indeed, as the pin enters the skin the patient shows no signs of pain. The person under hypnosis then may be asked to imagine a blackboard and to write certain words on it. He may then be told that he cannot recall the words. Later, he may be told that he can recall the words. With changing commands, most patients respond exactly as they are told. The hypnotist may tell the patient that he can see something that is not actually present, or he may be told he cannot see something that really is present.

Is Hypnosis a Trick? (continued)

Some people can respond to a large variety of commands, but most people can only be influenced to do a limited number of things. In no instances can they be influenced to do things that are distasteful or dangerous to them. In other words, a hypnotist cannot change a bad person into a good citizen or transform a good human being into a criminal.

Hypnotic Successes and Failures

Hypnosis has been most successful in calming people's fears and in helping them overcome bad habits. If an individual is afraid of flying or going to the dentist, his anxieties may be soothed through hypnosis. Hypnosis may also be very useful if a patient is overwhelmed by worries or fearful about discussing certain **perplexing** problems. In addition, patients have been successfully assisted in overcoming drinking and smoking habits.

Some hypnotists have claimed that they could get people to recall happenings from their former lives. A famous book called *The Search for Bridey Murphy* **allegedly** traced the life of an Irish girl back to a previous life. Investigations by scientists proved that this claim was not true.

Some crime investigators have experimented with hypnosis as a way of getting suspects or witnesses to reveal information (a little like a lie detector test). Unfortunately, an uncooperative witness can easily resist hypnosis. Even cooperative witnesses may report highly inaccurate information unintentionally. Hypnosis is not helpful in the search for the truth.

If you want to try your hypnotic skills, find a friendly dog and see if you can put him to sleep. Calm him down, lie next to him in the grass, and yawn 100 times. If the dog is not startled by activities around him, he may begin to yawn, too. Don't expect your yawning trick to last very long.

Questions and Discussion

1. Describe the sequence of steps a hypnotist is likely to use in hypnotizing a patient.

   _____
   _____
   _____

2. If you were describing the work of a hypnotist and you wanted the audience to understand the decisions she has to make, what sequence of decisions would you outline? (For example, she has to first decide who would make a good subject.) List three other decisions in the right order.

The Man with the Magic Touch

Words you'll need to know...
imaginative can think of new ideas
ingenious very clever and skillful
inventive can develop new things
poverty poor people, poor farms, and businesses

Have you ever had a friend or known somebody who could figure out clever ways of solving a problem? Perhaps you needed money for a project, and he or she suggested several ways of earning the money. Perhaps you needed to create a story, a bulletin board, or a play, and your friend seemed to have an endless supply of great ideas. We usually call these people **imaginative**, **inventive**, or **ingenious**.

One of the most imaginative and skillful people in America was born into slavery as a tiny baby. Shortly after his birth, he was kidnapped by masked horsemen in the middle of the night. He didn't know what was happening to him, of course, but he soon must have realized that his mother was gone. His old master is said to have traded a race horse to get the baby back.

The baby, George Washington Carver, grew up on a farm near Diamond Grove, Missouri, during the Civil War. As soon as he could talk, he began to ask about the plants he saw around the farm. He quickly learned how to care for them. He was so skilled that he became known as "the plant doctor."

After the war was over, the slaves were free. This allowed George Washington Carver to go to college. He studied at both Simpson College and Iowa State College. He cleaned buildings, washed laundry, and cooked in order to pay his college costs. Carver was so brilliant as a student, however, that he was asked to join the faculty as an assistant after he graduated.

In 1896, when few African Americans even went to school, Carver was already a research scientist. He saw so much **poverty** in the southern part of the United States that he decided to help the farmers who grew cotton, peanuts, pecans, and sweet potatoes. Carver developed hundreds of new uses for the crops they grew. He made 300 products from peanuts and 118 products from sweet potatoes. He even made starch, gum, and wallboard from cotton stalks. With so many new uses, the farmers' crops were in much greater demand.

Carver was quickly recognized both in the United States and Europe. He was given many awards, and a monument was dedicated to him on the Missouri farm where he was born. Not many people have come from such simple beginnings and achieved so much!

Questions and Discussion

1. See if you can put the events in George Washington Carver's life in the correct order. Mark the statements below with number 1 for the first event to number 6 for the last event.

   _____ a. Carver helped the farmers.

   _____ b. Carver gained his freedom.

   _____ c. Carver was kidnapped.

   _____ d. Carver went to college.

   _____ e. Carver became known as "the plant doctor."

   _____ f Carver was given many awards.

2. If it was raining and you were going to a wilderness area to establish a camp, in what order would you probably carry out these tasks? Mark number 1 through number 5.

   _____ a. Look for firewood.

   _____ b. Put up the tent.

   _____ c. Find a source of clean water.

   _____ d. Find a dry place to pitch the tent.

   _____ e. Build a fire.

3. If you came upon a serious car accident, in what order would you do these three tasks? Mark them as 1, 2, and 3.

   _____ a. Stop the bleeding of victims.

   _____ b. Call 911.

   _____ c. Get a passing motorist to warn traffic away from the accident.

Booker T. Washington

Have you ever wondered whether your personality and your life would have been different if you had a different name? If your first name were Stone instead of Charles would people treat you differently? If a girl were named Cleopatra instead of Jane would people think of her in a different way?

Booker T. Washington, one of the greatest black leaders in the United States, had the interesting task of naming himself. He was born a slave. Slaves either had only one name or they took the name of their owners as their last name.

When Washington was freed with the rest of the slaves, he was just known as Booker. At a mission school, he noticed that other students had two names. Since he was to be enrolled, the teacher asked for his last name. Booker simply said "Washington" because he had heard of George Washington. Little did he know that he would soon make the name Washington famous again.

Booker T. Washington had a difficult life as a child. As a slave and after he was free, he had to work from an early age. He worked in a coal mine for nine months of the year, but he was allowed to attend school the other three months.

Washington attended Hampton Institute and later taught there. He realized that education was very important, and he wanted to make certain that African Americans had opportunities to learn. He founded what is now Tuskegee Institute in 1881. At the time, there was one teacher and fifty students. Twenty-five years later, under Washington's leadership, Tuskegee had 1,500 students and a full list of courses.

Thousands upon thousands of African Americans have benefited from their education at Tuskegee Institute.

Questions and Discussion

1. Booker T. Washington's life involved many events. See if you can number them in the order in which they occurred.

    _____ a. Tuskegee's enrollment reaches 1,500 students.

    _____ b. The slaves are freed.

    _____ c. Washington works in the mines.

    _____ d. Washington gives himself the last name of Washington.

    _____ e. Washington graduates from Hampton Institute.

    _____ f. Washington establishes Tuskegee Institute.

2. Suppose you were planning a party for your friends. List the tasks you would have to complete and the order in which you would do them.

UNIT 5
Selecting Criteria FOR USE IN MAKING JUDGMENTS

Words you'll need to know...

criteria guidelines or rules to check how good something is
durable strong; will last a long time
impulsive acting without careful thought

What we think is good, valuable, or worthwhile depends on the criteria we use. When we select **criteria** for use in making decisions, we develop or choose standards. These standards help us decide which clothes or food or pets or friends we like best. If you want a pet that is easy to care for, you might choose a goldfish. If you want a pet that is fun, you might buy a kitten or puppy.

We often have to make hard choices. Amy had a limited amount of money for clothes. However, she really wanted a jacket for skiing. Amy's parents urged her not to simply get the first thing that caught her eye. Her parents wanted her to choose carefully and get something she could wear for a long time. Put a check beside the three **criteria** Amy ought to watch for and use in buying her new jacket.

_____ 1. Is the jacket strong and **durable**?

_____ 2. Will the colors in the jacket fade or run together?

_____ 3. Will her friends like her jacket?

_____ 4. Is the jacket an attractive and noticeable color?

_____ 5. Is the jacket washable?

(You should have a check beside 1, 2, 4, and 5.)

Many people enjoy hobbies. They may collect coins or stamps or raise animals for 4-H. They may build model railroads or camp in the woods. Some prefer art activities or carpentry. If you were choosing a hobby, what criteria would you consider most important? (cost, whether you have friends who have the same hobby, whether the hobby requires learning new and difficult skills, etc.) Write two criteria on another sheet of paper that you would consider most important.

A friend has probably asked you why you bought a specific game or joined a particular club at school. You may have had to admit that you didn't really think about it very much. This could mean that you are not making very wise choices. You may be **impulsive** rather than thoughtful about what you do. You can probably improve your life by using criteria in thinking through your choices.

The Great Escape

Words you'll need to know...
bowie a large knife

If we're young and we cause trouble our parents may ground us. They may tell us we can't leave the house or they may even require us to stay in our bedrooms. Police officers do much the same thing with criminals who break the law.

During the Civil War, there was a very daring general from the South. He caused a lot of trouble for President Lincoln and the Union Army. This general, John Morgan, led only a few thousand men on horses but they could strike like lightning. They would circle around behind Union lines, burning bridges, stealing horses and supplies, and destroying buildings.

At one point, General Morgan and his men crossed the Ohio River into Indiana. A flood caused the river to rise, and Morgan could not get back to southern territory. Morgan and 69 of his men were captured and put in the Ohio State Penitentiary.

The Ohio State Penitentiary was like a fortress. It had strong walls. The guards had dogs, and there was an alarm system.

Shortly after Morgan was placed in his prison cell, he noticed that the dirt floor of the cell was dry and free from mold. He decided that there must be a tunnel or open space underneath the floor.

Morgan and his cellmates began digging through the dirt. Men from the next cell scooped up the dirt and hid it in mattresses. Finally, the men uncovered the walls to an underground tunnel. They cut through the wall with large **bowie** knives that they had kept hidden. The tunnel led to an area inside the high walls that surrounded the prison grounds. From their tunnel hideout, they cut through a five-foot inner wall, twelve feet of clay, and a six-foot-thick outer wall.

On a stormy night in November of 1863 Morgan and his men quietly cut the rope to the alarm bell, slipped beneath the wall, and disappeared into the darkness. They had gained their freedom by cutting through almost 25 feet of dirt, brick, and cement. Fortunately for the North, General Morgan was later defeated in Kentucky.

Questions and Discussion

1. Assume you are building a prison from which you don't want anyone to escape. What two criteria would you consider most important? Check two.

    _____ a. Keep the prisoners as happy as possible so they don't want to leave.

    _____ b. Build the prison far out in open fields or on an island.

    _____ c. Don't allow visitors.

    _____ d. Keep lots of guard dogs.

    _____ e. Have big search lights everywhere.

    _____ f. Check all the cells every two hours.

2. You are buying new clothes. What two criteria will you use in making your choices (style, color, care, cost, etc.)?

    _____
    _____
    _____

3. You want to buy a new car. What two criteria would you consider most important (purchase price, size, color, style, gas mileage, etc.)?

    _____
    _____
    _____

4. You are thinking of joining a school club. What two criteria would be most important (size of the club, club activities, membership cost, whether you have friends already in the club, etc.)?

    _____
    _____
    _____

5. Your sister wants to buy a plant for her bedroom. She has asked you for suggestions. You want to raise questions that will allow her to choose wisely. What two criteria would you stress the most (cost of plant, how fragile it is, how much care it requires, what flowers it may have, etc.) List the two criteria you would stress.

    _____
    _____
    _____

Teaching the Big Cats

Words you'll need to know...
ancestors parents and grandparents
ferocious ruthless and savage
galloping very fast-moving animals
pedestal a pillar that can hold something on top of it
prey animals that are eaten by other animals

You may have tried to teach a puppy to sit up. You may also have attempted to get a kitten to use the litter box. The puppy will usually learn more quickly because its **ancestors** had to follow the lead dog in a pack of wolves. Cats, on the other hand, are much more independent. They don't like to follow a leader.

People throughout history have tried to train wild animals to do tricks. Cleopatra, the famous queen of Egypt, and her son kept many wild animals. They used them in parades. They also taught them to sit up and beg for food.

More recently, we have had exciting animal trainers, such as Gunther Gebel-Williams, who has used lions, tigers, leopards, elephants, and horses in the same acts. This is very difficult because some, like lions and tigers, are natural enemies. Others, like horses, are natural **prey** for the big cats. Lions, tigers, and leopards often weigh three times as much as a large man and they have enormous strength. They can also strike with lightning speed.

In his act, Gebel-Williams enters the arena standing up on a **galloping** horse. He holds a flaming torch in one hand. He then jumps from the back of the horse and begins to put the most **ferocious** animals on Earth through their paces. The big cats leap from **pedestal** to pedestal. They sit up, roll over, play dead, and jump through flaming hoops.

Training wild animals is extremely dangerous! Over the years, wild animal trainers have suffered from deep bites and huge scratches. One early trainer, Clyde Beatty, was bitten so badly that doctors thought he would lose his leg. On another occasion, a lion struck his gun and caused it to go off against his body. It set him on fire. The lion backed off. Then Beatty's assistant threw a bucket of water on Beatty and put out the fire.

Animal trainers tend to use similar ways of controlling the wild animals they teach. They usually hold a whip in one hand and a chair in the other hand. They crack the whip over the heads of the animals and sometimes fire blank shots from a pistol. They keep the chair between themselves and the beasts they are facing. Clyde Beatty once controlled 50 lions and tigers in a cage at one time. It was so tremendously dangerous that he never tried it a second time.

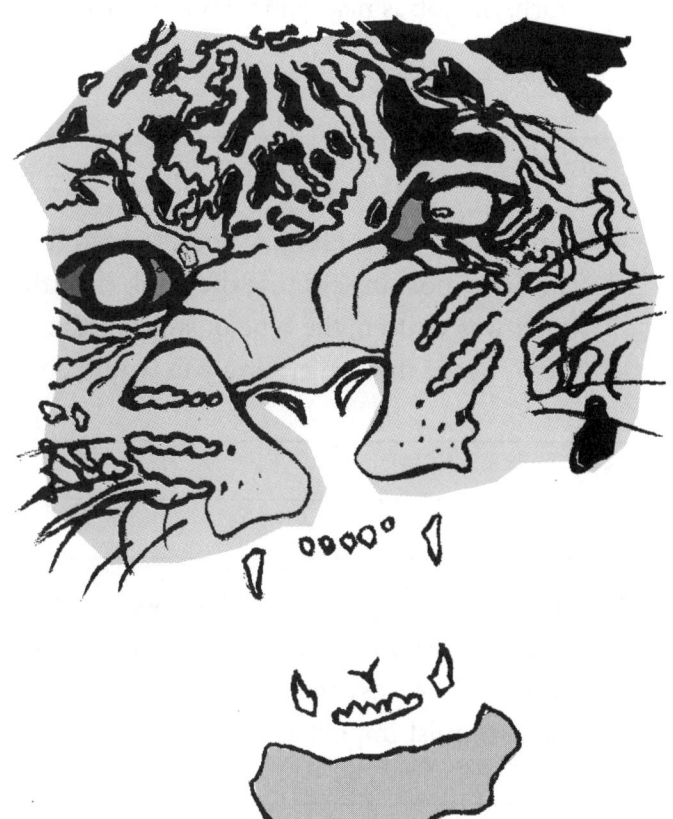

SELECTING CRITERIA FOR USE IN MAKING JUDGMENTS

Questions and Discussion

1. If you were selecting big cats for a new show, what three criteria would you consider most important (the cats are beautiful, the cats have performed before, the cats get along with other animals, the cats were not caught in the wild, they are willing to obey the trainer)? Write your three choices.

_____
_____
_____

2. Your friend is choosing between two brands of sneakers. What two criteria do you think are most important (cost of sneakers, durability of material, can they be worn for various activities, are they washable)? What two criteria are most important? Write them below.

_____
_____
_____

3. You are looking for a summer job. What two criteria would be most important (good pay, pleasant work, you have friends working there, you can sleep late before work, the job is near your home)? List the two most important considerations.

_____
_____
_____

4. You are choosing a library book to read for English class. What would you consider most in selecting the book (length of the book, the time period when the book was written, the type of story in the book, how difficult the book is to read, etc.)? Write the two criteria you would consider most important.

_____
_____
_____

5. You are in charge of preparing food for a school party. What would you consider most important in selecting the food (cost of the food, whether the food is popular, how easy the food is to prepare, how nourishing the food is, etc)? Write the two most important criteria below.

_____
_____

Survival in the Arctic

Words you'll need to know...
ice floes islands of floating ice
summit the highest point
wastes areas with no plants

Have you known people who always wanted to take chances? If there was a high fence they wanted to jump over it. If there was a deep river they wanted to dive into it.

Naomi Uemura (oo-YEH-moo-ruh) was this kind of bold and fearless adventurer. He looked for dangerous challenges all over the world. He climbed the highest peaks in North America, South America, and Africa. He floated over 3,600 miles down the Amazon River. He climbed Mount Everest with the first group of Japanese to reach the **summit**.

Uemura had a brush with death when he fought his way to the forbidden areas of the North Pole. He had prepared carefully for the trip. Uemura had polar bearskin pants, a fur-lined parka, and sealskin boots. He also had rich red meat, biscuits, and coffee, along with dog food. He arranged to have additional food dropped from airplanes.

It was -49 degrees Fahrenheit when he started out from northern Canada. Despite the brutal Arctic cold, things went well at first. Then Uemura ran into huge ridges of ice. He often had to smash a hole through solid ice and jump between **ice floes**. He had to float his sled in the water as a bridge so the dogs could run to the other side. This was dangerous because no person or animal can live if they fall into Arctic water. They will freeze to death.

The fourth night out was the worst. As Uemura bedded down in his tent he heard the dogs frantically yapping. The frightened animals chewed through their leashes and ran wild. Then he heard a bear as it tore open his supplies. Uemura had a rifle but it was not loaded. He lay still as the bear poked Uemura in the back, tore a hole in the tent, and left.

Uemura radioed for new supplies, collected his dog team, and loaded his rifle. As expected, the polar bear returned for a second meal. Uemura quickly shot him. As the long hard days wore on, the cold grew more intense. He was eager to reach the Pole before other threatening problems occurred. There was always the possibility that he or the dogs would slip into the frigid water. There was also the danger of freezing to death in your sleep.

Finally, after 55 days and 476 miles of brutal Arctic weather, Uemura stood at the North Pole. He had accomplished something no other person had ever achieved. He traveled by himself across the frigid **wastes** to the Pole and lived to tell about it!

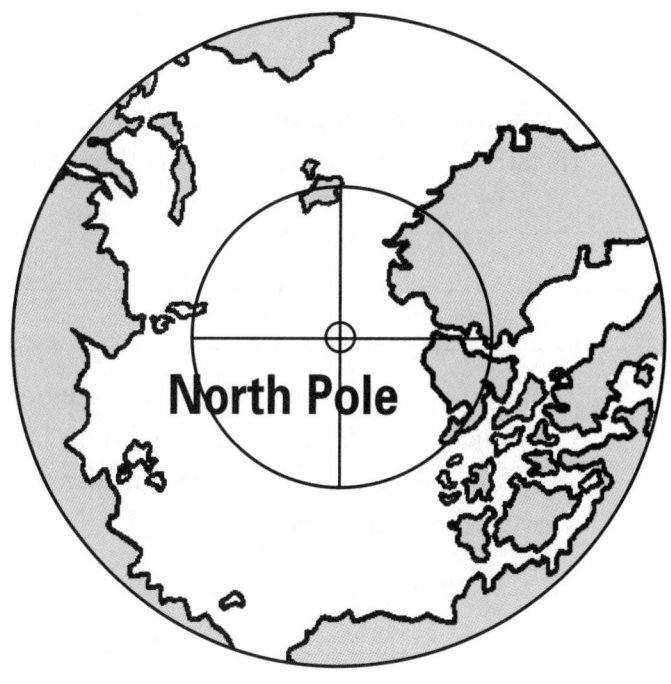

Questions and Discussion

1. If you were considering several possibilities for an adventurous trip, which two criteria listed below would you consider important? Put a check beside your two choices.

    _____ a. The trip would include other people.

    _____ b. There would be a rescue plan in case of serious problems.

    _____ c. There would be money donated to pay the costs of the trip.

    _____ d. The trip could help provide important scientific information.

    _____ e. The trip would take you to places you had never seen before.

2. If you were planning to get a pet, what aspects of cost and care would you consider most important?

    _____
    _____
    _____

3. If you were choosing people for a basketball or soccer team, what skills and personal characteristics would you consider most important? List two of each.

    _____
    _____
    _____

4. If you were choosing an apartment, what would you consider most important factors (location, size, cost, etc.)? List the three most important criteria for you.

    _____
    _____
    _____

5. You have moved to a new town. You are hoping to find a good friend. What three characteristics would you feel were most important? (They are wealthy, they are loyal, they are popular, they consider education important, they are good at sports.) List your three choices.

    _____
    _____
    _____

Dangerous Superhuman Achievements

Words you'll need to know...
endurance strength that continues over a long time
innocence not guilty
perform complete a task
souls inner spirits

Coach Garcia called his team to the sideline. Something had to be done. If the other team kept scoring, the Panthers would never catch up. Garcia fixed his eyes on the players and growled, "If you don't think you can win, you're going to lose every time."

Coach Garcia was right, of course. If we assume that we can't accomplish something, we often fail. If we feel defeated before we start, we may not really try. On the other hand, we have read about people in emergencies who have shown enormous strength and **endurance.** They have lifted cars off people trapped underneath. They have run long distances to get help. And they have even carried injured people for miles to find medical assistance.

Many of the fire walkers of Europe and Asia seem to be able to protect themselves from being burned. In most cases, a shallow trench is filled with red hot coals. The fire walker then runs from one end of the trench to the other. This shows that they are "masters of fire."

The fire walkers **perform** these daring acts for several reasons. Some are holy men who want to show that they have special powers. Some want to purify their **souls** or show their **innocence.** Still others want to please the gods so they will have a good harvest.

Scientists have examined the feet of many fire walkers before and after they walk on the hot coals. The scientists suspected that the fire walkers had put chemicals on their feet or taken drugs to relieve their pain. Some investigators thought that fire walkers might have added extra water to their feet (hydration). Extra water could protect against some of the burning. So far, there seems to be no agreement about how successful fire walkers protect themselves.

It is obvious that many fire walkers are not "masters of fire." An article in *Natural History* (June 1974) describes how 10 out of 15 fire walkers in India at the time were severely burned. This happened in the village of Sunderpur and it led many of the local people to believe that their gods had abandoned them.

Only one thing seems certain. As long as people walk on fire, some will be successful and others will fail. We may never know why there is a difference.

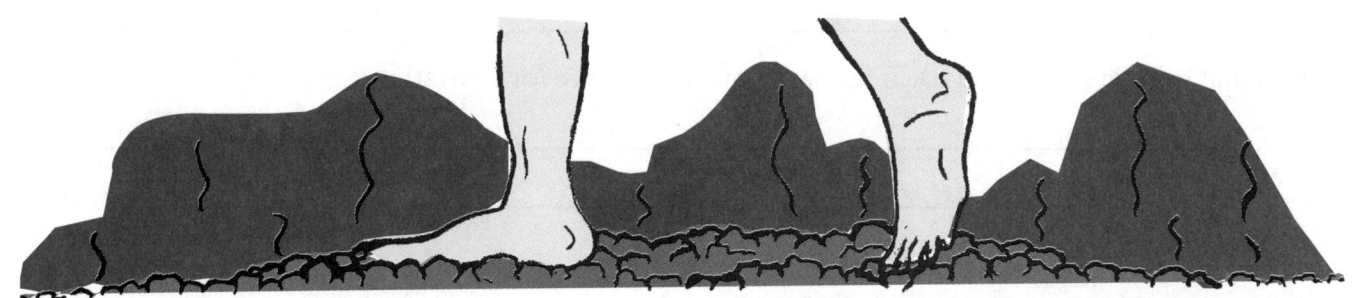

SELECTING CRITERIA FOR USE IN MAKING JUDGMENTS

Questions and Discussion

1. What criteria would you use to select people for a group to explore a jungle area? Choose two.

   _____ a. People who are healthy.

   _____ b. People who can tell good stories.

   _____ c. People who have explored before.

   _____ d. People who do not have pets.

2. What criteria would you use to choose a game for a long rainy afternoon? Choose two.

   _____ a. A game that involves kicking a ball.

   _____ b. A game everybody will enjoy.

   _____ c. A game that uses very little space.

   _____ d. A game that takes a long time to play.

3. If you were going to pick a baby-sitter to watch your little brother, what criteria would you use in making your choice?

   _____
   _____
   _____

4. If you were buying a car, what criteria would you use in making your selection?

   _____
   _____
   _____

5. What criteria would you use if you were buying a tent for camping?

   _____
   _____
   _____

6. What criteria would you use if you were picking a place for a vacation?

   _____
   _____
   _____

An Indian Woman Leads the Way

> **Words you'll need to know...**
> **Shoshone** the name of an Indian tribe
> **Wyoming** the name of a large western state

If you ever became lost in the woods, you probably wondered how you could find your way home. Do you follow a stream? Do you watch to see where the sun is setting? Do you search for animal trails? Do you watch for smoke from campfires?

Explorers throughout history have had to watch for signs in nature so they could find animals and plants for food, clean water, and sheltered places to spend the cold winter months.

Probably no explorer ever walked and paddled boats farther than Meriweather Lewis and William Clark. They were sent by President Jefferson in 1804 to explore the Louisiana Purchase. They knew very little about the land they were exploring. After they left St. Louis, it took them a year and a half to reach the Pacific Ocean. They battled snowstorms. They became sick from a constant diet of fish, boiled roots, and stewed dog meat. They feared Indian attacks. They ran so short of food that they finally had to eat their horses.

A young Indian named Sacajawea (Sak-uh-juh-WEE-uh) helped save the group several times. Sacajawea was married to one of the French guides. She was a **Shoshone** who was captured by the Minnatsaree Indians five years earlier. She knew the Pacific Northwest well and guided the group through dangerous passes. She convinced other Indians that the trip was one of peace. She used her knowledge of nature to find food in the wilderness. Sacajawea even got her brother, a Shoshone chief, to provide horses. All of this she did while caring for and carrying her newborn baby.

According to one story, Sacajawea died in 1812 a few years after the group returned East. There was, however, an old Indian woman living in **Wyoming** in 1875 who claimed that she was Sacajawea. She told a convincing story of the famous Lewis and Clark trip. If she was the real Sacajawea, this woman would have been close to 100 years old at the time of her death.

SELECTING CRITERIA FOR USE IN MAKING JUDGMENTS

Questions and Discussion

1. If you were limited in what you could take with you into a strange region, what would you emphasize? (Communication equipment such as a radio, first aid supplies, arms to protect yourself, extra food and clothing, waterproof maps, flashlights, books about the region, etc.) Write the two you feel would be most important.

   _____
   _____

2. If you had an opportunity to choose between two concerts, what criteria would you use to decide? (You might pick the most famous band, you might select the singer you like best, you might choose the biggest band, you might pick the band that has the best staging.) Write the two criteria that would be most important to you.

   _____
   _____

3. What criteria would you use in selecting a camping site? (A site protected from the wind, a site near your friends, a site near restroom facilities, a site near an outside security light, a site on high ground.) List the two criteria you would select.

   _____
   _____

4. You are planning to buy a dog. What would be most important to you? (A friendly dog, a dog that doesn't shed fur, a dog that obeys you, a dog that other people will admire, a dog that doesn't cost very much.) Write the three criteria you would emphasize the most.

   _____
   _____

5. You are going to learn a new craft such as sewing or wood-carving. What would be most important to you? (Materials are inexpensive, you can make things as gifts, you can use your crafts around your home, the skill you develop is one that few people have.) Which two criteria do you think are most important? Write them below.

   _____
   _____

Adrift in the Atlantic Ocean

> **Words you'll need to know...**
> **containers** cans or bottles to hold something
> **flares** a signal that burns
> **inspiration** something that gets people excited and gives them hope
> **lure** attract
> **torpedoed** blew up a ship with an explosive

Have you ever wondered what you would do if you had little food and water? Would you be willing to eat grass or insects? Would you know how to find water?

Many people have survived by catching rain water and eating squirmy little things that hide under rocks. However, the record for endurance probably belongs to a Chinese sailor named Poon Lim.

Poon Lim was a sailor aboard the British merchant ship, the *Ben Lomond*, in 1942. During World War II a German submarine **torpedoed** the *Ben Lomond* 565 miles off the coast of central Africa. As the ship sank, Poon Lim jumped from the burning deck into the ocean. He wore a life jacket that kept him afloat.

Poon Lim soon found a life raft and climbed aboard it. On the raft, he found a tin can of fresh water, several **containers** of biscuits, a flashlight, and several **flares**. With these simple supplies, Poon Lim drifted across the Atlantic Ocean for 133 days.

It wasn't long before his fresh water and biscuits were gone. At this point, Poon Lim had to think of other ways of getting food and water. He used his life jacket to collect rain water to drink. He took the wires out of his flashlight and made fish hooks. He cut the insides out of the fish he caught to **lure** sea gulls to his raft. When the gulls landed, he grabbed them and used them for food as well.

On April 5, 1943, Poon Lim saw a fishing boat and got the attention of the men on board. The crew of the boat welcomed him, but he could not understand their language. Poon Lim had floated all the way across the widest part of the Atlantic Ocean. The men who rescued him were Brazilian sailors from South America.

Soon the news of his rescue spread around the world, and the United States Congress granted him citizenship. Doctors could not believe that a person could survive for so long without better food. Poon Lim lost only 20 pounds and he was strong enough to walk ashore without assistance. His courage and clever problem solving saved his life and served as an **inspiration** to others.

Questions and Discussion

1. If your ship sank in the ocean and you had three rafts to choose from, what criteria would you use in selecting your raft? What would be the most important?

2. If you were buying a horse to ride a long distance, what criteria would you use in choosing your horse?

3. You want to impress a person you want to date. What would be the most important things to emphasize? List three below.

4. You would like to be chosen for a sports team. What criteria do you think a coach uses in selecting people for the team? List three below.

5. You want to impress a potential employer. What criteria do you think she will use in judging you? List three below.

Inventing a New Language

Words you'll need to know...
Cherokee a tribe of Native Americans
dedicated serious and eager about something

Have you ever tried to use hand signals or codes to communicate with your friends? Sailors sometimes use flags to send messages. Short-wave radio operators can communicate over long distances. Telegraph operators use dots and dashes to make up words.

It is not difficult to send one word like "Help" or a few words like "Take the dog out." But if you are trying to invent a whole new language it is a huge task.

A **Cherokee** named Sequoya (sih KWOY uh) invented a written language for his people. He did it all by himself.

Sequoya was born in eastern Tennessee in 1760. As a teenager he tried many things. He made silver ornaments, he hunted deer, and he caught animals for their fur. Unfortunately, he was badly injured in a battle. His leg wounds made it difficult for him to walk.

Sequoya turned his attention to studying the Cherokee language. There was no alphabet for Cherokee. His friends could only talk together. They could not write letters, prepare agreements, or keep records of tribal happenings.

Sequoya listened to the sounds in his language and developed an alphabet of 86 letters to represent the sounds he heard. It took him 12 years of hard work. After all of this work, he still had to teach people in his tribe how to read the new written words.

Finally in 1828, there were enough people who could read Cherokee to allow the printing of a newspaper called the *Cherokee Phoenix*. The reports in the paper were in Cherokee and English.

Leaders in Washington soon realized that Sequoya was a very talented and **dedicated** man. They worked with him in developing peace treaties and agreements.

Seqouya was recognized for his enormous achievements. A forest of huge trees in California was named after him. The state of Oklahoma sent a beautiful statue of him to the Capitol Building in Washington, D.C. It is displayed to this day in Statuary Hall.

SELECTING CRITERIA FOR USE IN MAKING JUDGMENTS

Questions and Discussion

1. What criteria would you emphasize if you were trying to make up a new code or language? (The code is easy to learn, the code can be used in the light or the dark, the code allows you to send long messages, the code can be sent by sound or sight, the code has signals that are not easily mixed up.) Write the two criteria you think are most important.

   _____
   _____
   _____

2. What criteria would you use in selecting entertainment for your friends? Write two below.

   _____
   _____
   _____
   _____

3. Suppose you are baby-sitting and needed to think of ways of entertaining preschool children. What criteria would you use in selecting activities? Suggest two criteria.

   _____
   _____
   _____

4. A friend of yours has asked you to help him select a gift for his mother's birthday. What criteria would you suggest? List two below.

   _____
   _____
   _____

5. A cousin has asked you to come to her farm to visit for two weeks in the summer. You can't take all of your clothes, of course. What criteria will you use in selecting the clothes you do take? Write two criteria below.

   _____
   _____
   _____
   _____

SELECTING CRITERIA FOR USE IN MAKING JUDGMENTS

The First Worldwide Automobile Race

> **Words you'll need to know...**
> **mechanics** people who fix machines
> **Seattle** a city on the northwest coast of the United States
> **vague** unclear

The drivers and **mechanics** in the first worldwide automobile race spent months trying to get their cars across the United States, Russia, and Europe. It took them 169 days to travel the 13,340 miles from New York City to Paris, France.

By 1908 manufacturers in Germany, France, Italy, and the United States had developed automobiles that were fairly dependable. The Germans had produced a 60-horsepower vehicle called the Protos. The Americans also had a 60-horsepower car called the Thomas Flyer. The Italians and French had 40 horsepower and 12 horsepower cars.

The New York to Paris transcontinental race began on February 12, 1908. More than 200,000 people gathered excitedly in Times Square, New York. This may have been the craziest race in history. The drivers had only a **vague** idea of where they were going. There were almost no roads, maps, or road signs, and very few gas stations outside the big cities. It was extremely cold and there were few hotels or restaurants on the plains and in the mountains. South of the Great Lakes the snow was so deep that the driver of the American car paid $1,000 to have 10 teams of horses drag sleds to pack down the snow for 100 miles. The road across Iowa was nothing but a ribbon of mud two feet deep in places.

The drivers had brought food and medicine, extra clothing, guns, shovels, spare parts, and tools. These items were helpful, but they weren't useful when the motorists were lost in the mountains.

The Pacific Ocean presented a huge challenge! The driver of the American car hoped to save time by taking a ship to Alaska and driving across the ice on the Bering Strait to reach Russia. He did not know that the water in the Strait never freezes hard enough to hold weight. The plans were quickly changed. All of the cars sailed from **Seattle** to Russia.

Once the drivers reached Russia, they were again faced with simple cow paths for roads and almost no places to get food and gasoline. In fact, they couldn't even speak the language. The American car got lost in the mountains and wasted two days. The driver used the stars and a compass to find his way back to the route. The German car reached the Russian capital of St. Petersburg first. The Russian ruler (called the czar) was impressed and awarded the driver $1,000.

The final part of the journey was the easiest because the roads were better. The American car quickly took the lead. It arrived in Paris first. The Italian car reached Paris two weeks later. Only three of the six cars that started the race actually arrived in the French capital. They had accomplished what few people had dreamed possible. They proved that the automobile was here to stay.

Questions and Discussion

1. What criteria would be most important to you if you were choosing an automobile race to enter? (The race is not very long, you get to ride with friends, you know the territory where you are going, the weather is good.) Write below the two criteria you feel are most important.

   _____

   _____

   _____

2. If you were choosing a game for little children to play, what criteria would you keep in mind? Write three below.

   _____

   _____

   _____

3. What criteria would you use if you were selecting a skit to perform? Write three below.

   _____

   _____

   _____

4. If you were selecting a new pair of shoes what criteria would you emphasize? Write two below.

   _____

   _____

   _____

5. What criteria would you use in selecting a gift for a friend in the hospital? List two below.

   _____

   _____

   _____

UNIT 6
Detecting ASSUMPTIONS

It is a weekday morning. You are dressed, you've eaten your breakfast, you've collected your books, and are running out the

> Words you'll need to know...
> **assumption** something that is thought to be true
> **speculate** guess

front door. The neighbors may assume that you are going to school. All the things they see you doing would lead them to believe that it is a regular school day for you. If, on the other hand, you are dressed in a baseball uniform this might lead the neighbors to assume that you are leaving to play ball.

In many situations, there is evidence that so clearly leads to certain conclusions that we can make **assumptions** with confidence. If there is a clerk behind the counter in a store, we can reasonably assume that the clerk is employed by the store. In other instances, there are so few clues that we may be bewildered and confused. We don't know what to assume. Perhaps you are in your car behind a long line of cars on a highway. You wonder if there has been an accident. You may **speculate** about flooding on the road, highway construction, or the possibility that there is a police checkpoint. Since you can't see far enough down the road to detect what is happening, you can't make an assumption with confidence. If an ambulance comes by, however, you may be inclined to assume that there has been a problem involving the health and safety of people on the highway.

Assumptions often control the way we react to situations. Several young children of American military families in Germany went trick-or-treating on Halloween. As usual, they knocked on doors, held up sacks, and called "trick-or-treat!" One German woman was later heard to say that she really didn't want any of the candy the child offered but he seemed so insistent that she finally took some. The little boy learned all too quickly that he and the German woman were assuming different things.

Dr. William Mann of the Washington National Zoo was attempting to capture small game and snakes for the zoo. However, he found that the natives were so accustomed to hunting animals for food that the captured animals were disappearing as fast as they were caught. He finally persuaded his helpers that he wanted the animals kept alive. The natives assumed that hunting and eating went together. One of the reasons we have problems with assumptions is that we don't consider the possibility of other explanations. Try to think of other explanations for the following situations.

Questions and Discussion

Your brother assumes that his table lamp won't work because the bulb is burned out. What other explanation could there be?

_____
_____
_____
_____

A child in a shopping cart is crying. You think he hurt himself. What other explanations could there be?

_____
_____
_____
_____

It is even harder to detect the assumptions of the writer when we read articles and reports. The author of the report will seldom tell you what he is assuming. He'll simply take these assumptions for granted and move on with his recommendations. Look at the proposals below.

1. After we eliminate the wolves from Yellowstone Park we will open more areas to campers. What is the writer assuming?

_____
_____
_____
_____

2. When the heat lets up we'll see more animals coming out of the woods. What is the writer assuming?

_____
_____
_____
_____

The Most Misunderstood Animal in the World

Words you'll need to know...
commotion loud movement or noise
deadliest something that can cause you to die
fascinating exciting or very interesting

It is a shame that most people hate and fear snakes. We weren't born that way. We learned to fear snakes from the things other people say.

When we avoid snakes, we miss out on one of the most **fascinating** creatures on Earth! Even though snakes have no legs, they can climb trees, move quickly across the ground, and swim. They can go without food for a year or more. They can also expand their jaws to swallow animals that are two or three times the size of their own heads. As they grow larger, they actually shed their skins.

Believe it or not, snakes are our friends. They eat mice and rats that destroy many of our best crops. Scientists have estimated that one snake may eat as many as 300 mice during a year.

Most snakes are not poisonous. In the United States there are some poisonous rattlesnakes, copperheads, and water moccasins. They don't attack people unless they are disturbed. It is easy to avoid them. They like to keep to themselves.

Some people actually keep snakes as pets. Most people keep non-poisonous snakes. Peter Snyman has been a snake collector for many years. On six occasions he has been bitten by his poisonous friends but lived to tell the story.

After learning that the *Guinness Book of World Records* had a report of a man who lived with poisonous snakes for 36 days, Snyman decided to try to beat the record. He collected two dozen cobras, six black mambas, six puffadders, and six South African boomslangs.

Snyman knew that he had to remain quiet. Quick movements might startle the snakes and cause them to attack him. Snyman spent hours in frozen silence. His companions crawled all over him. The curious snakes inspected his nostrils, ears, and eyeglasses.

Snyman was allowed to leave the cage for thirty minutes each day to eat, use the bathroom, and wash. The most dangerous part of his stay was when there was a **commotion** outside the cage. This caused one of the black mambas to strike Snyman's pillow. It left a stain of venom where Snyman's head had been earlier.

Snyman finally left the cage unharmed after 50 days. He had beaten the world record!

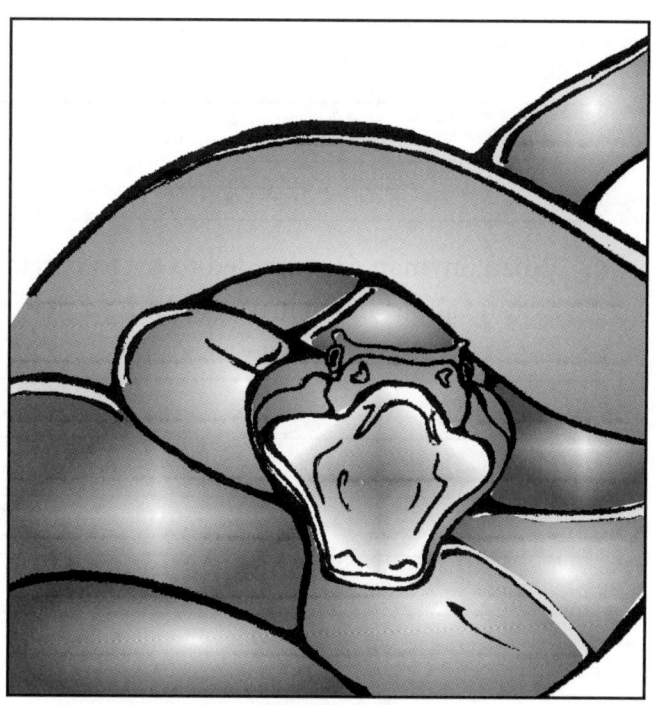

Questions and Discussion

1. What do most people probably assume when they see a snake in a field or woods?

2. What did Snyman assume regarding his movements in the cage and the likelihood he might be bitten?

3. Snyman had some friends outside the cage with antivenin medicine at all times. What did Snyman assume about the quickness with which the medicine might be needed?

4. When Snyman first decided to try to break the old record, what did he probably assume about his chances of setting a new record?

Dealing With Stress

Words you'll need to know...
anticipate foresee, expect
determination strong will or intention
dominate keep under control
frustrating disappointing, preventing one from reaching a goal or desire
hassled troubled, bothered
strategies careful plans
taunt put down or mock

When Glenn Cunningham was eight years old he was severely burned in a schoolhouse fire. He spent months lying in bed. Doctors said he would never walk again. The doctors must not have known about the young boy's **determination**. Glenn not only walked again, he learned to run as well. In 1934 he ran the mile faster than any human being on Earth! Glenn Cunningham would not let his tragic problems get him down!

Douglas Bader loved to fly airplanes. Unfortunately, he lost both legs in a crash. His country, England, was under attack from Germany. Bader had two artificial legs made and then joined the Royal Air Force to fly a fighter plane. The Germans captured Bader on three occasions but, even though he had artificial legs, he escaped every time.

James E. West was a crippled boy living in a children's home. He was sad and lonely much of the time. His life didn't look very promising but like Glenn Cunningham and Douglas Bader he didn't give up. He became the first president of the Boy Scouts of America.

There are no perfect methods of getting rid of stress, but there are excellent ways of dealing with these difficulties. Many of the problems you face can be reduced through careful planning and thoughtful decision making. Tensions that could easily **dominate** your thinking for a whole day or a whole week can be dealt with more intelligently. Sometimes you can do something to reduce the problem. Sometimes you can do something to change your attitude or your reaction to the problem.

Nine Strategies for Dealing With Stressful Problems

1. *Don't quit too soon!* Daniel Goleman, the author of *Emotional Intelligence*, says that we often cheat ourselves by deciding very quickly that we can't play sports, draw, write short stories, or act in plays. We reject each activity because we don't feel successful the first time we try it. There are millions of people who were not good when they started, but many of them didn't simply quit. Like Glenn Cunningham and Douglas Bader, they kept trying.

2. *Don't be afraid to express your concerns.* You are likely to feel much less stress when you believe things are fair. Speak up if your classmates leave you with all the clean-up duties following a party. People need to share responsibilities as well as fun. If you are riding with a driver who is going too fast, tell him or her you are worried. The driver has no right to risk your life!

3. *Avoid social situations that cause stress.* There is no reason for you to accept the **taunts** and insults of other students. Ask to change your seat or move to other tables in the cafeteria to avoid being **hassled**. **Frustrating** relationships with others can increase your stress.

4. *Make sure that you are prepared for class or work each day.* When you are unprepared, you

anticipate failure. The expectation of failure increases stress.

5. *Avoid making decisions when you are tired and upset.* You are likely to overreact. When you are tired, things seem worse than they really are.

6. *Try to find a close friend.* Everybody needs a good friend, someone who cares about you and is loyal to you. When you feel pressured, misunderstood, or abused, it is very comforting to share your frustrations with a close friend. It may be your mother or father, a neighbor, a sibling, or someone at school. In any case, a caring friend who knows how to listen can be a great help when you need to unload your feelings.

7. *Exercise.* Thousands of people have found that unused energies stored up while they are worrying can add to their nervousness and anxiety. The body's reaction to highly stressful situations is known as the "fight or flight" response. The body is ready for action. If there is no opportunity to act, this frustrating situation may cause headaches, an upset stomach, or additional tension.

8. *Set personal goals but don't try to do everything at once.* Some students make plans that are far too complicated and demanding. Then they find themselves overwhelmed. Find out how long it takes you to read ten pages, do six math problems, or write one page of a report or story. Then allow enough time to complete your work.

9. *When you can't get a stressful problem off your mind, don't panic.* Remind yourself that you have faced problems all your life and you are still here. Problems tend to fade with time. Frustrations that appeared to be overwhelming a few short weeks ago may seem unimportant as you look back on them later.

Questions and Discussion

1. What might a neighbor have assumed if they knew Douglas Bader immediately after his plane accident? Put a check beside the best answer.

    ___ a. Bader would be flying again very soon.

    ___ b. Bader would join the Royal Air Force.

    ___ c. Bader would recover fully.

    ___ d. Bader would be very discouraged.

2. What might a friend have assumed he if saw Glenn Cunningham after the schoolhouse fire?

    ___ a. Glenn would be back in school shortly.

    ___ b. Glenn's parents would put him up for adoption.

    ___ c. Glenn would win an Olympic medal.

    ___ d. Glenn would feel sorry for himself.

3. A person living in Florida states that unless truck traffic is reduced the highways will need to be replaced. What is this person assuming? Write your answer on another sheet of paper.

4. After a neighbor observes holes in his yard, he says he will have to get rid of his dogs. What is the neighbor assuming? Write your answer on another sheet of paper.

5. A friend tells you that if you don't buy the coat in the window, you'll have to wear your old coat. What is he assuming? Write your answer on another sheet of paper.

6. A politician states that we can either spend all our money on arms or be conquered by our enemies. What is she assuming? Write your answer on another sheet of paper.

7. A friend tells you, "If you want to go to a movie, fine. Otherwise, there is nothing to do." What is she assuming? Write your answer on another sheet of paper.

Can Dreams Predict the Future?

Words you'll need to know...
lucid very clear, very real
nightmares frightening dreams
tragic event a very sad, shocking happening

In 1865, Abraham Lincoln was sleeping in the White House when he dreamed that he heard people crying downstairs. In the dream, Lincoln saw himself go down the stairs where he saw a coffin. In his dream a soldier tells him that the body in the coffin is that of the president. A few days later Lincoln was killed. Was the dream a warning?

In 1912 a young girl dreamed that the ship *Titanic* was sinking. A few hours later news came that the *Titanic* had, indeed, sunk. Many passengers died after it hit an iceberg. Was the girl's dream a warning?

Throughout history some people have thought of dreams as messages from God. Native Americans thought dreams predicted the future. The Iroquois Indians believed that dreams revealed the wishes of supernatural beings. The Sioux Indians even sent young boys out alone into the desert to encourage dreaming. When the boys returned, they told about their dreams and older men would then explain what their future careers would be. The boys might become warriors, hunters, priests, artists, or medicine men.

Scientists have been studying people's dreams for many years now. They have learned that everybody dreams. Babies have dreams even before they are born. Cats, dogs, and blind people also dream. Most people dream several times during a night's sleep. Some dreams are pleasant and other dreams are frightening. Some people dream very little.

Studying dreams is very difficult for scientists because people often have a hard time recalling the details of their dreams. They become mixed up or confused. Their explanations are hazy and puzzling. The people who describe their dreams are not always very definite or clear about what actually happened.

Scientists have found out that there are several kinds of dreams:

1. Some dreams are lucid. During a **lucid** dream you realize it is a dream while it is happening.
2. There are waking dreams or daydreams. Your eyes are open but your mind is wandering. You may be thinking of happenings in the past or future.
3. There are **nightmares**. These are scary dreams in which you may be chased or threatened. You usually wake up feeling upset or frightened. Nightmares happen more often when you are sick or under great pressure.
4. Finally, there are creative dreams. Dreams allow your thoughts to move all over the place. These dreams aren't restricted to things that make sense. Several writers, including Robert Louis Stevenson, believed they got many of their best story ideas from their dreams.

One writer who couldn't make her characters interesting even forced herself to dream by filling her mind with questions. That night she dreamt of a house with crooked walls, a crooked roof, crooked floors, and crooked windows. Suddenly, she realized that her characters were too nice; they needed to be more crooked. This would make them more interesting to the reader.

Today, scientists believe that dreams are of our own making. Dreams come from our everyday experiences—from things we worry about, from our fears about the future. If we hear or read about a **tragic event** in our community we may dream that something similar is happening to us.

Was Abraham Lincoln's dream a warning? Was the little girl's dream about the *Titanic* really a message about the ship?

Probably not. Many people have dreamed about their possible deaths. Few large ships have ever left for sea without someone believing they may not return.

Dreams, however, do tell us things about ourselves. If you have nightmares regularly you may want to learn to relax. You may want to stop worrying about bad things that will probably never happen to you.

Questions and Discussion

1. If a scientist studying dreams interviews you and says, "Tell me about your dreams," what is he assuming? Check the best answer.

    ___ a. He is assuming that your dreams are all happy ones.

    ___ b. He is assuming that you want to describe your dreams.

    ___ c. He is assuming that you have nightmares.

    ___ d. He is assuming that you have dreams.

2. A friend tells you that there won't be anything to do if you don't join the Boys' Club. What is he assuming? Write your answer below.

    _____

    _____

3. A schoolmate states, "If we had two more players, we could have won the game." What is she assuming? Write your answer below.

    _____

    _____

4. A soccer player says that if the team isn't ranked number one, it might as well not be ranked at all. What is the player assuming? Write your answer below.

    _____

    _____

5. A friend says that he is going to exercise more because he wants to be healthy. What is he assuming? Write your explanation below.

    _____

    _____

6. A mother tells you that she is buying her child an encyclopedia because she wants him to graduate. What is she assuming? Write your answer below.

    _____

    _____

7. A doctor explains that the school area will need to be cleaned in order to avoid sickness. What is the doctor assuming? Write your explanation below.

    _____

    _____

Giants of the Deep

Words you'll need to know...
gauge a tool to measure something
prey animals that are eaten by other animals

Sally Johnson lives along the sunny coast of Florida just north of Miami. There is a colorful blue and white marina across the street from her home. On pleasant days sleek fishing boats glide in and out of the sparkling harbor searching for schools of ocean fish. Some of the sports fishermen chase giant white sharks. These 20 foot, 5,000–pound eating machines often follow cruise ships and gulp down the garbage as it is thrown overboard. They seem to have an endless appetite.

Popular adventure movies such as *Jaws* depict giant white sharks as man-eating monsters. The movies lead us to believe that an unsuspecting swimmer is a shark's favorite food. There is no question about the fact that sharks have attacked swimmers. According to the Shark Attack File at the Florida Museum of Natural History, there have been 245 recorded shark attacks on people since 1876. Sixty-four of these resulted in death. However, scientists who study the behavior of sharks now believe that great white sharks spit out people after they attack them.

Peter Klimely, a scientist at the University of California Bodega Marine Laboratory, says, "No one has ever shown me a situation where the entire body of a person was taken out of a shark's stomach." Klimely believes that sharks are picky eaters. They really don't want to eat people. Shark attacks on people are simply mistakes.

Klimely's research team has carefully observed 128 white shark attacks on all kinds of sea animals. Klimely found out that the sharks prefer blubbery seals, sea lions, and whales to birds, otters, and humans that have much less fat.

Klimely believes that since white sharks are warm-blooded and constantly in motion, they may need a high-energy diet to survive. They cannot afford to fill their stomachs with lean meat. That would be like an Olympic athlete trying to gain energy by eating lettuce.

Although we may think that sharks are surrounded by food, they really have to work to catch their **prey**. In the 1990s Klimely got a large female shark to swallow a temperature **gauge**. This would indicate when she ate. They tracked the shark for days as she swam around the ocean in an unsuccessful search for food. Finally she caught a seal. When sharks do catch food they often warn other sharks away with a special kind of tail-splashing signal. They don't want other sharks to steal their supper!

Remember! Sharks don't want to eat you, so don't make it easy for them. They might mistake you for a seal.

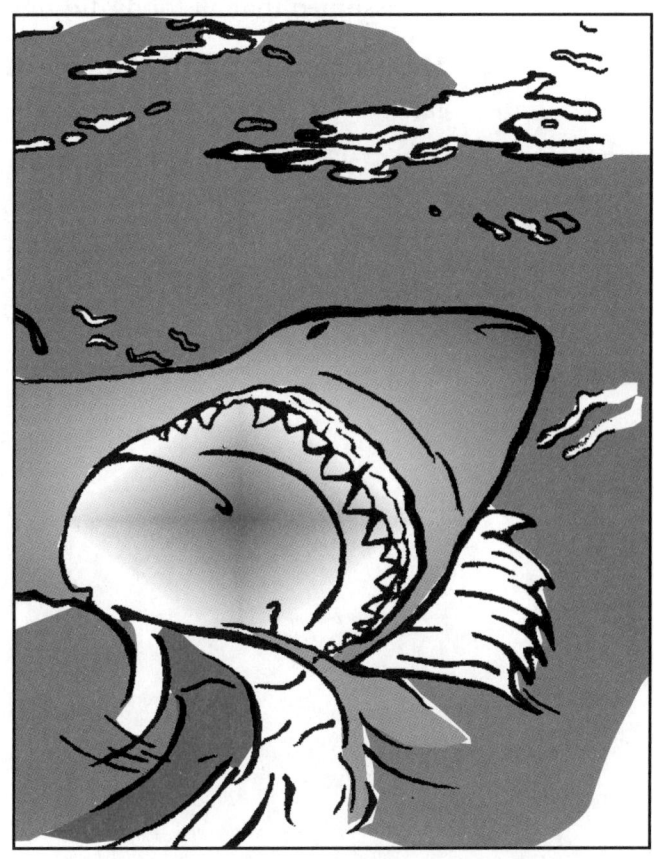

Questions and Discussion

1. What did Klimely probably assume when he first started studying sharks? Mark the best answer.

    ___ a. He assumed that the sharks would like to be studied.

    ___ b. He assumed that he and his team could learn about sharks by observing them.

    ___ c. He assumed that sharks did not attack people.

2. When Klimely got the female shark to swallow the temperature gauge, what did he assume?

    ___ a. He assumed that the shark would spit the gauge out.

    ___ b. He assumed that the shark would quit swimming.

    ___ c. He assumed that when the shark swallowed food, the gauge would register a change in temperature.

3. What did Klimely assume about a shark's ability to tell one food from another?

    ___ a. He assumed that they only eat one kind of animal.

    ___ b. He assumed that all foods did not taste the same to sharks.

    ___ c. He assumed that sharks would prefer animals that have lots of blubbery fat.

Ballooning to the North Pole

> **Words you'll need to know...**
> **dynamite** a powder used in explosives
> **survival** to keep on living

A little over one hundred years ago several explorers were competing with each other to be the first to reach the North Pole. Most traveled by ship. One Swedish explorer, Salomon Andree, attempted to make the trip by balloon. He quit his job and started raising money to pay for his journey. King Oscar II of Sweden and Alfred Nobel, the inventor of **dynamite**, provided the needed funds.

A huge balloon was purchased. It had a basket beneath it that could carry three people and their supplies.

On July 11, 1897, Andree and two companions lifted from the ground. They caught a gentle breeze and sailed toward the North Pole. After they had traveled one-third of the way (250 miles), the three men ran into fog. Ice began to form on their balloon. On July 14 they crashed.

Andree felt that their only chance of **survival** would be to travel by foot overland to Spitsbergen. They killed polar bears after their limited supplies of food ran out. On October 5th they reached White Island. It was 50 miles from Spitsbergen. They set up camp. Their diary notes ceased that same month.

No one discovered what happened to Andree and his two companions over the next 33 years. Finally on August 5, 1930, Gunnar Horn of Norway and several seal hunters found their frozen bodies. They also uncovered their journals and rolls of film. Surprisingly, the film was developed successfully. It recorded the events of their tragic trip.

Questions and Discussion

1. What did Andree assume about the strength of the balloon?

   _____

   _____

2. Since the three men took very few supplies, what did they probably assume about the length of their trip?

   _____

   _____

3. Since Andree and his companions set out for Spitsbergen, what did they probably assume about that trip?

   _____

   _____

DETECTING ASSUMPTIONS

A Simple "No" That Started A Revolution

Words you'll need to know...
bonds money paid to get temporary release from jail
discrimination an act based upon prejudice
fares money paid to ride a bus, train, plane, or subway

Have you noticed what happens when a person quietly stands up for his or her rights? Have you watched when a friend has refused to give up something that is rightfully his or hers? When people recognize that they are fighting for justice, not just selfish interests, they often seem to find tremendous strength.

On the evening of December 1, 1955, a frail forty-two-year-old African-American woman named Rosa Parks was seated in the front of a city bus. A white man asked her to give up her seat so he could sit. Parks was very tired after a long day's work. She knew that black people were supposed to ride in the back of public buses but she felt the rule wasn't fair. The bus driver told Parks to move but she refused.

The bus driver threatened to have her arrested. Parks replied, "Have me arrested. I'm not going to move." The bus driver called to policemen at the next stop. Parks was then taken to the Montgomery city jail, fingerprinted, and booked. She could get out of jail only if someone paid her one hundred dollars **bond** money.

Within two hours more than fifty people came to the jail to pay for her temporary release. Parks was then able to go home where her worried husband and mother were waiting.

Parks's trial was set for the following Monday. She was found guilty of breaking the law and fined. Both white and black people in Montgomery were disturbed with the court's decision. After all, this is the Land of the Free! What kind of justice required black people to give up their seats to white passengers?

The black citizens of Montgomery decided to refuse to ride the buses. Nearly empty buses meant that the bus company didn't collect **fares**. Without riders, the bus company soon went broke. Shortly after this, the Supreme Court of the United States ruled that "**discrimination** on buses was a violation of federal law."

Although Rosa Parks did not believe that she was doing anything very important, her belief in justice and her personal courage resulted in a whole new world for African-American citizens.

80 DETECTING ASSUMPTIONS

Questions and Discussion

1. What did the man who requested Parks's seat assume Parks would do? Check the best answer.

    ___ a. He expected her to ignore him.

    ___ b. He expected her to share her seat.

    ___ c. He expected Parks to move.

    ___ d. He assumed Parks would refuse.

2. When laws are written and passed, what do most people assume? Check the best answer.

    ___ a. They assume the laws are not fair.

    ___ b. They assume the laws will be ignored.

    ___ c. They assume the laws will be enforced.

    ___ d. They assume the laws will be changed.

3. What does a driver probably assume if he is speeding? Write your answer below.

    _____
    _____

4. What are you likely to assume if you are taken to court? Write your answer below.

    _____
    _____

5. What does the judge assume if you are given a fine? Write your answer below.

    _____
    _____

6. If you are found guilty of a crime, what can you assume? Write your answer below.

    _____
    _____

7. If a law is found to be unenforceable, what might we assume? Explain your assumption below.

    _____
    _____

DETECTING ASSUMPTIONS

Review:
PUTTING IT ALL TOGETHER

- Recognizing Sequences
- Identifying Assumptions
- Classifying Ideas, Objects, People, and Events
- Drawing Valid Conclusions
- Selecting Criteria for Use in Making Judgments
- Recognizing the Difference Between Facts and Opinions

Faithful Forever

Words you'll need to know...
Greyfriars a church in Edinburgh, Scotland

Bob and John were never apart. They lived in the same house; they ate in the same dining room; they slept in the same bedroom.

Unfortunately, these close friends were separated by death. John Gray was buried in the **Greyfriars** churchyard in Scotland in 1858. Bob watched sadly as his friend was lowered into the ground.

When services were over, the minister and John's other friends left, but Bob remained by the newly dug grave.

Later that evening, Bob was still at the graveside. His head was bowed and he was very quiet.

"Come home with us," friends urged.

Bob did leave but he did not stay away long. The next morning, he was missing; he had gone back to the grave of his friend. There he lay quietly as though he expected his devoted companion to return at any time.

Others took an interest in Bob. He would leave for a short period but then he would go back. Some tried to reason with him, but Bob did not understand or seem to care.

Bob never did go back to his old house. Finally, he was allowed to stay at Greyfriars church. The neighborhood children brought him food and water. Sometimes when the weather was very bad, a person might bring a shawl to cover him. Once a bronze medal was made for him to wear because he was so loyal. Bob stayed on and on. He stayed for 14 years, never moving but a short distance from the spot where he last saw his friend.

Then one morning in 1872 he was found very quiet and still at the side of the grave. He was motionless and peaceful. Bob was buried nearby so he and his friend could be close together.

Today, in Candlemakers' Hall in Edinburgh, there is a fountain. It was built to honor Bob. Bob was a dog, a dog who never deserted his master.

Recognizing Sequences

1. Number the events below to indicate the order in which they occurred in the story.

    _____ a. Bob was allowed to live at Greyfriars church.

    _____ b. People tried to reason with Bob.

    _____ c. A fountain was built to honor Bob.

    _____ d. John Gray died.

    _____ e. Bob was buried near his master.

Identifying Assumptions

2. The people of Edinburgh made an assumption regarding what Bob would do after John Gray died. What did they probably assume?

___
___
___
___

Classifying Ideas, Objects, People, and Events

3. Animals and people can be wonderful friends, yet scientists classify them differently. Place the characteristics below under the correct headings.

> They can make plans for the future, their babies are helpless for several months.
> They need few comforts to survive, they usually need body coverings.
> They can talk, they can exist in the wild.

People	Animals
_____	_____
_____	_____
_____	_____

Drawing Valid Conclusions

4. It is not always easy to draw conclusions about animal behavior because animals don't think the same way we do. What do you think is the safest conclusion to draw regarding Bob's behavior at the grave?

___
___
___
___
___

REVIEW 85

Selecting Criteria for Use in Making Judgments

5. If you were selecting a dog for a pet, what criteria would you use? (behavior, size, health, etc.)

   _____
   _____
   _____
   _____
   _____
   _____
   _____

Recognizing the Difference Between Facts and Opinions

6. Write *fact* before statements below that are factual and *opinion* before those statements that express opinions.

   a. _____ Bob was a good dog.

   b. _____ Bob lay near the grave for years.

   c. _____ Dogs should find new owners.

   d _____ Bob was given a medal.

   e. _____ People noticed Bob's loyalty.

   f. _____ Bob would still be at the grave if he hadn't died.

   g. _____ The neighborhood children brought Bob food and water.

The Song That Wrote Itself

Words you'll need to know...
eerily frightening and ghostly
mist fog or haze

As you know, our country suffered terribly through a long and tragic civil war. Thousands of soldiers died from battle wounds, sickness, and prison conditions. Wives and mothers waited anxiously for news of their husbands and sons.

On the night of November 18, 1861, fog was drifting up from the Potomac River. Long lines of soldiers shuffled wearily through the dingy streets.

A red-haired woman sat by the window of her darkened room. She watched the marching troops. Campfires showed **eerily** through the **mist**. The gaslight on the corner gleamed on gun barrels. Mrs. Julia Ward Howe was moved by the scene. She was weary from a long train ride, but late that night she sat at her desk. She wrote a poem that stirred the whole nation.

The next morning Howe studied her poem. She remembered nothing of what she had written. The name of the poem was "The Battle Hymn of the Republic." A little while later, it was published in a magazine.

Charles McCabe, who was a prisoner in a Confederate jail, happened to get a copy. He noticed it could be sung to the tune of "John Brown's Body." McCabe and his fellow prisoners heard about the Union victory at Gettysburg. To celebrate, they sang the song.

Later, McCabe told a theater audience about the experience. He sang the song. The audience sang it. President Lincoln rose to his feet with tears in his eyes.

Julia Ward Howe said, "I feel that I did not write it. I was just a messenger. It really wrote itself!"

Recognizing Sequences

1. Number the events below to indicate the order in which they occurred in the story.

    _____ a. The poem was published in a magazine.

    _____ b. Charles McCabe sang the poem "The Battle Hymn of the Republic" to the tune of "John Brown's Body."

    _____ c. Julia Howe took a train trip.

    _____ d. Julia Howe wrote a poem.

    _____ e. Charles McCabe heard about the victory at Gettysburg.

Identifying Assumptions

2. Howe could not remember writing "The Battle Hymn of the Republic" so she assumed that it wrote itself. What do you think really caused her to think this?

_____
_____
_____
_____

Classifying Ideas, Objects, People, and Events

3. Look at the items listed below, and classify them as either fighting equipment or sporting equipment. Some can be placed in both categories.

rifles, tents, ammunition belts, boots, cannons, knapsacks, mess kits, fishing poles

Sporting Equipment   **Fighting Equipment**

_____   _____
_____   _____
_____   _____
_____   _____

Drawing Valid Conclusions

4. "The Battle Hymn of the Republic" refers to the North and the Union soldiers fighting for truth. How valid do you think it is to suggest that truth was on one side and not the other? Give your reaction below.

_____
_____
_____
_____
_____

Selecting Criteria for Use in Making Judgments

5. If you were selecting soldiers, what physical, mental, and social traits would you stress?

   _____
   _____
   _____
   _____
   _____
   _____
   _____

Recognizing the Difference Between Facts and Opinions

6. Write *fact* before statements below that are factual and *opinion* before those statements that express opinions.

   a. _____ Many lives were lost in the Civil War.

   b. _____ "The Battle Hymn of the Republic" is a great song.

   c. _____ President Lincoln heard the song.

   d. _____ There was a victory at Gettysburg.

   e. _____ Mothers and wives were fearful.

   f. _____ Fighting the war was a bad idea.

   g. _____ The war started in 1861.

A Magic Trick

Words you'll need to know...
audience people who watch or listen to a show
magician person who does tricks
props objects used on stage during a show

Many of us would love to be a **magician**. We could entertain our friends, and we would look as if we had special powers. A simple trick is described below that you can do for any fairly large group of people.

First you write the name of a person in the **audience** on a piece of paper and seal it in an envelope. Then you give the envelope to someone to hold. Next you ask people in the audience to call out their first names. As the names are called, you write on small slips of paper and put them in a paper bag. After this, a volunteer draws a name out of the paper bag and reads it aloud. Finally, the person holding the envelope opens it and reads the name written on the slip of paper. It is the same name that has been drawn from the bag.

How is this done? It is very simple. The magician writes the same name as that in the envelope on all the slips of paper put in the bag. The magician makes sure that the name in the envelope is called out, of course. Otherwise the trick won't work.

People in the audience will wonder how you managed to match the name since the envelope was not opened until the very end.

Recognizing Sequences

1. Number the directions for doing the trick in the proper order.

   _____ a. No matter what names are called out, the magician writes down and puts the same name in the bag that has been put in the envelope.

   _____ b. The magician asks the audience to call out their first names.

   _____ c. The magician asks someone to draw a name from the bag and read it.

   _____ d. The person holding the envelope is asked to open it and read the name. It is the same name that was drawn from the bag.

   _____ e. The magician writes the name of someone in the audience on a piece of paper, places the paper in an envelope, and seals it.

   _____ f. The magician gives the sealed envelope to someone in the audience.

Identifying Assumptions

2. As the magician hears names called out from the audience and writes on small slips of paper, what does the audience assume?

   _____

   _____

Classifying Ideas, Objects, People, and Events

3. Many performers have **props** to help make their shows more interesting. See if you can classify the things listed below that are props and those that are not props.

   > chairs for the audience, makeup, costumes, scenery, ushers, footlights, printed programs

   Props   Not Props

   _____   _____
   _____   _____
   _____   _____
   _____   _____

Drawing Valid Conclusions

4. A few people in the audience might watch your trick and conclude that you have magical powers. What could you do to persuade them that this is not a valid conclusion?

Selecting Criteria for Use in Making Judgments

5. We have all attended shows that were exciting. We have also gone to shows that were uninteresting. What criteria would you suggest that would help people plan more interesting shows? Would a fast-moving program or one with surprises be best? Would you want programs with audience participation? Write your ideas below.

_____
_____
_____
_____
_____
_____
_____
_____

Recognizing the Difference Between Facts and Opinions

6. Put *fact* before the statements below that are factual and *opinion* before those statements that express opinions.

   a. _____ Magic tricks are hard to do.

   b. _____ Magic tricks have been around for many, many years.

   c. _____ Magic appeals to everybody.

   d. _____ Magic should not be seen by little children.

   e. _____ Magic is a good form of entertainment.

   f. _____ Magicians do not need musicians in order to perform.

The Man With the X-Ray Mind

Words you'll need to know...
skeptical not believed, questioned
Westminster Abbey a church in London, England

Scotland Yard, the famous police center in England, was having no luck in finding the missing Stone of Scone. The stone had been stolen from **Westminster Abbey** in December 1950. Finally, they decided to call in Peter Hurkos.

A Scotland Yard officer and Hurkos flew to London. Hurkos went to the Abbey. The police let him examine a tool and a wristwatch left by the thieves. He also studied the food scraps left by the thieves, and Hurkos then slowly traced on a map of London the path taken by the burglars as they hauled the stone away.

He had never been to London before but he described the buildings along the route he had traced on the map. He also described the thieves. He said there were three men and a woman. When they were captured three months later, they fit the descriptions Hurkos had given exactly.

The police in Nijmegen, Holland, also used Hurkos's help. In August 1951 the city and countryside were hit by dozens of fires. More than 200 officers patrolled the area, but fires continued to burn barns, houses, and bridges. One night Hurkos was walking along a street with a friend when suddenly he said, "Another fire will soon break out. It will be at the farm of a family named Janson." The two men hurried to warn the police and learned the fire had just been reported.

Hurkos told the police he could help them, but they were **skeptical**. Shutting his eyes, he described what was in the police captain's pockets. After this, the police believed he could help.

First Hurkos went to the fire scenes. Digging through the ashes, he came up with a charred screwdriver handle. He felt it and said, "We must look for a boy in his teens." Hurkos was shown the school yearbook pictures of every boy in town. He finally pointed to a photograph. "That one!" he said. "That is the one I want to talk to."

He had named the son of one of the richest people in town. Hurkos said, "You will find a box of matches in one pocket and a bottle of lighter fluid in the other, but the boy doesn't smoke."

The boy denied everything. Then Hurkos said, "Pull up your left pant leg and show the police the scratches you got from the barbwire fence as you ran from the fire!" The scratches were there. The boy confessed. Later, he was sent to a mental institution.

Recognizing Sequences

1. Number the events below to indicate the order in which they occurred in the story.

   _____ a. A Scotland Yard officer and Hurkos fly to London.

   _____ b. Hurkos seeks to find the person setting fires.

   _____ c. Hurkos traces on a map of London.

   _____ d. Hurkos goes to the Abbey.

   _____ e. Scotland Yard is looking for the Stone of Scone.

Identifying Assumptions

2. When Scotland Yard officers called Hurkos to help, what did they probably assume?

   _____
   _____
   _____
   _____
   _____
   _____

Classifying Ideas, Objects, People, and Events

3. In police investigations, people are often classified as innocent, suspects, or guilty. Place the individuals listed below in each category.

   > bystander, person seen driving the guilty person, person seen carrying out the crime

Innocent	Suspect	Guilty
_____	_____	_____
_____	_____	_____
_____	_____	_____
_____	_____	_____

94 REVIEW

Drawing Valid Conclusions

4. When Hurkos shut his eyes and described what was in the police captain's pockets, the officers came to the conclusion that Hurkos could help them. Do you think this was a valid conclusion? Explain your reasons below.

_____
_____
_____
_____
_____
_____

Selecting Criteria for Use in Making Judgments

5. If you were choosing a new police officer, what criteria would you use in making your selection?

_____
_____
_____
_____
_____
_____

Recognizing the Difference Between Facts and Opinions

6. Put *fact* before the statements below that are factual and *opinion* before those statements that express opinions.

   a. _____ The police need the help of Peter Hurkos.

   b. _____ The police were grateful for Hurkos's help.

   c. _____ The boy setting the fires was mentally disturbed.

   d _____ The burned screwdriver belonged to the boy who set the fires.

   e. _____ The boy had scratches on his left leg.

   f. _____ Peter Hurkos helped the police solve crimes.

   g. _____ Peter Hurkos was very observant.

Bicycling Across the English Channel

Words you'll need to know...
albatross seabird that can fly long distances
chariot a fancy wagon with two wheels pulled by animals
gossamer very, very thin cloth
muscle-powered driven by people's bodies

Long before we saw the bicycle rider in *ET* sail across the screen, people dreamed of soaring with the birds. Our ancestors in ancient lands imagined **chariots** surging across the sky. Several even tried attaching wings to their arms. In recent years, a man who raised Canadian geese led his flock south for the winter. Popular magazines showed pictures of him flying his small ultra-light plane surrounded by excited geese.

About forty years ago, a British businessman named Henry Kremer offered a large award to anyone who could fly a **muscle-powered** aircraft a certain distance. They were to follow a figure-eight-shaped course that covered three miles.

Hundreds of athletes and mechanics tried to win the prize. Kremer urged them on by increasing the prize to well over $100,000. Finally, in 1977 a medal-winning bicyclist and a glider champion from California tried for the prize. Bryan Allen, the bicycle champion, invented an odd-looking airplane and practiced flying it for several weeks.

To make it around the three-mile course the plane had to almost float on its own while Allen's frantic peddling pushed it forward. The odd plane, therefore, had to have a huge wingspan of 96 feet (wider than some commercial airliners). It also had another wing on a pole out in front to steady the aircraft. There was, of course, a seat and pedals. There was also a long bicycle chain that drove a 13-foot propeller in the rear. The entire plane weighed only 77 pounds, far less than most adults weigh.

After 400 test flights, Allen and his partner Paul MacCready took the funny-looking plane to a field near Bakersfield, California. Allen pedaled the craft down the runway and into the air. The plane never got higher than 12 feet off the ground. It only flew for seven and a half minutes, but Allen completed the three-mile course. Later that day MacCready and Allen walked away with Henry Kremer's generous prize. The achievement was important enough for the strange plane to earn a place in the unusual aircraft display at the Smithsonian Institution in Washington, D.C.

Shortly after Allen and MacCready successfully met the three-mile challenge, Henry Kremer offered a much more difficult venture. He offered twice as much money to anyone who could complete a muscle-powered flight across the English Channel. This would be a gigantic achievement! Instead of three miles, it would be twenty-three miles over water with normally gusty winds.

MacCready and Allen decided to accept the new challenge. They knew they would need to design and build an entirely new aircraft. It would need to be stronger and easier to handle. MacCready and Allen worked with the DuPont Company to find lighter, stronger materials. In the end, they were able to build a better plane that was only 57 pounds, 20 pounds lighter than their first plane.

MacCready and Allen knew that weather could ruin everything. They shipped their new craft named the **Gossamer Albatross** to England and waited. A month went by before a windless day occurred.

On June 12, 1979, the *Gossamer Albatross* was moved to the end of a special wooden runway that led to the edge of the channel. Allen climbed into his seat, but as the plane rolled down the ramp, a wheel broke. The wheel was quickly replaced. The second attempt was successful. Moments later the *Gossamer Albatross* lifted off. Allen pedaled furiously and leveled the craft off just 15 feet above the water. Below were two rescue boats and a third boat with news reporters.

The trip presented several problems. At one point a large tanker ship approached, and Allen had to change directions. Shortly thereafter a head wind arose and the *Albatross* slowed. As it did, it dropped to within six inches of the water. Allen quickly brought it back up. The heat inside the *Albatross's* thin covering rose so high that Allen thought he might faint.

Allen's legs began to cramp, but he could see the faint shoreline of France in the distance. As he grew weaker, the coastline drew closer. Finally the water below gave way to sand. Exhausted but excited, Allen landed the *Gossamer Albatross* on the beach. The impossible had finally been accomplished! No one since that time has attempted to match this stunning record.

Recognizing Sequences

1. Number the events below to indicate the order in which they occurred in the story.

    _____ a. The *Gossamer Albatross* is moved to England.

    _____ b. MacCready and Allen consult with the DuPont Company.

    _____ c. The *Gossamer Albatross* is designed.

    _____ d. Henry Kremer offers a reward for three-mile course.

    _____ e. Allen's airplane is placed in a Smithsonian exhibit.

Identifying Assumptions

2. MacCready and Allen made an important assumption about their first aircraft before planning to accept the second challenge. What was the assumption?

    _____

    _____

    _____

    _____

    _____

    _____

Classifying Ideas, Objects, People, and Events

3. The *Gossamer Albatross* might be classified as both a bicycle and an airplane. Name three features that could classify it as a bicycle.

_____
_____
_____

Name three features that could classify it as an airplane.

_____
_____
_____

Drawing Valid Conclusions

4. We all know that people are timid or bold, unimaginative or creative, inclined to quit or persistent. What conclusions can you draw about MacCready and Allen?

_____
_____
_____
_____
_____
_____

Selecting Criteria for Use in Making Judgments

5. If you were choosing a person to fly the *Gossamer Albatross*, what criteria would you use in making your selection?

   a. _____

   b. _____

Recognizing the Difference Between Facts and Opinions

6. Put *fact* before the statements below that are factual and *opinion* before those statements that express opinions.

   a. _____ MacCready and Allen flew their plane near Bakersfield, California.

   b. _____ MacCready and Allen were brave.

   c. _____ The flight across the English Channel was a great achievement.

   d _____ MacCreadys and Allen's record will never be broken.

   e. _____ Henry Kremer was wise to offer a prize.

   f. _____ The first plane MacCready and Allen invented deserved to be placed in the Smithsonian Institution.

Cinque Wins His Freedom

> **Words you'll need to know...**
> **coastal ship** a boat that sails near land
> **United States marshal** a federal law officer

Like many people living in Africa two hundred years ago, Cinque was captured, enslaved, and was taken by ship to Cuba. In Cuba Cinque and the other slaves were freed of their chains and then put aboard the ship *Amistad*. The group was to be sent to another Cuban port.

During the voyage, Cinque and the other slaves seized control of the ship. The regular crew members were put in lifeboats and sent away. However, two of the original crew were kept to sail the ship back to Africa.

Cinque had the two experienced sailors take turns at the wheel. By using signs, he ordered them to sail the *Amistad* back to Africa. Instead, the sailors steered the ship to New York.

An American **coastal ship** sighted the *Amistad* and boarded it. Cinque dove overboard but was captured. The *Amistad* and the slaves were then turned over to a **United States marshal**. Cinque and his fellow Africans were charged with murder and piracy.

The blacks were put on trial, and they were defended by lawyers who were against slavery. The trial gained much attention because slavery was legal in America then. The case finally went to the Supreme Court of the United States in February of 1841. Ex-president John Quincy Adams argued the Africans' case. Finally the court decided that the blacks were not Spanish slaves or Spanish subjects but were free people.

Cinque and his friends toured the northern United States to raise money for a voyage back to Africa. The tour was a success. They were able to charter the ship *Gentlemen* and set sail for Sierra Leone, Africa, in December of 1841.

Cinque later worked at a Christian mission in Sierra Leone. He was never sorry for his actions on the *Amistad*. He said that he would do the same thing again if necessary. He was about 67 when he died.

Recognizing Sequences

1. Number the events below to indicate the order in which they occurred in the story.

    _____ a. Cinque returns to Africa.

    _____ b. Ex-president John Adams defends the Africans.

    _____ c. Cinque leads a mutiny on the *Amistad*.

    _____ d. Cinque tours the northern United States.

    _____ e. Cinque is captured in Africa.

Identifying Assumptions

2. What did Cinque assume when he directed the experienced sailors to steer the *Amistad* to Africa?

Classifying Ideas, Objects, People, and Events

3. In the early days of our history some people were classified as free and others were classified as slaves. How did Cinque's classification change from before he was captured until after he reached Sierra Leone?

Drawing Valid Conclusions

4. People are timid or brave, kind or cruel, inclined to quit or persistent, freedom-loving or frightened. What conclusions can you draw about Cinque?

Selecting Criteria for Use in Making Judgments

5. If you were preparing a list of criteria to use in choosing a captain for a ship, what would you list? (fun-loving, careful, kindly, smart, responsible, musical, a good athlete)

_____

_____

_____

_____

_____

_____

Recognizing the Difference Between Facts and Opinions

6. Put *fact* before the statements below that are factual and *opinion* before those statements that express opinions.

   a. _____ The *Amistad* was a ship.

   b. _____ The mutiny led by Cinque was wrong.

   c. _____ The Supreme Court made a good decision.

   d _____ Cinque could not steer the ship.

   e. _____ Cinque was wise not to try to steer the ship.

   f. _____ Cinque was a very brave person.